CONTENTS

BEATING THE BULLY

Recognising, Reporting and Empowering

Marianne Richards

Emerald Books

ISBN 978-1-84716-839-9

Series Editor Roger Sproston
Printed by 4edge www.4edge.co.uk

Typeset by Frabjous Books
www.frabjousbooks.com

Cover design by Creative Studios Derby

From Bullying

"The vast shipwreck of my life's esteems."
John Clare

*"The unexpressed urges that are not transformed
by positive action."*
Longfellow

To Empowerment

*"To bring to bloom the million-petalled flower
of being here."*
Philip Larkin

*"In an expanding universe, time is on the side of the outcast. Those
who once inhabited the suburbs of human contempt find.. they
eventually live in the metropolis."*
Quentin Crisp

*"When people do not want to see something, they get mad at the
one who shows them. The child is made to feel shame for bringing
shame to the family. But — did the child bring shame? No. The child
brought shameful things to light."*
Julie Cameron, The Artist's Way

*"**We can learn to find friends with whom we can safely vent pain**."*
Julie Cameron

To the memory of Tim Field
24th January 1952 – 15th January 2006
World anti-bullying expert & author of,
'Bully In Sight'

CONTENTS

LIST OF DIAGRAMS

WHAT THIS BOOK COVERS

This book is intended as an empowering guide for victims of bullying, families and supporters and also for bullies who want to reform. It is laid out in levels so information can be assimilated in order of importance. Thus, empowerment is first, followed by information on the major players, then human dynamics, history of bullying and snapshots of real life stories. This is the layout:

o Level 1 **empowerment** – rapid response to bully situations
o Level 2 **major players** – the roles people adopt in bully situations
o Level 3 **human dynamics** – links between thinking, feeling & behaving
o Level 4 **aggression, fear & anger** – what they are and how they link to bullying
o Level 5 **bullies through history** – perception of bullying over time
o **Perspectives** – stories of hope & encouragement
o **Resources** – books, film, organisations
o **Glossary**
o **Index**

The information in each level is subdivided into sections, numbered sequentially throughout the book from 1 – 45. At the head of each section is a bulleted list of what the section covers; UPPER CASE means the heading contains more than one item. At the end of each section is a bit of space for your own notes.

How to Use this Book
There are several ways of using this book.

1

- if you (or someone you know) is actively being bullied, concentrate on level 1 (empowerment) for advice / relief.
- For anyone under stress, who cannot assimilate a great deal of information, go through the book slowly, section by section (1–45). This will give a sense of achievement and mastery.
- For readers where the bullying has stopped who want an integrative self-training course, read level by level, comparing your experience with the information. It is useful to keep a Journal/diary of what you have learned before going to the next level.

Why I Wrote This Book

There is little public knowledge of group psychology (group dynamics) or how drastic changes of character happen in stressed environments. Nor do many people know how to define bullying or what bully, victim and bystander mean. Even those who need this knowledge rarely have it; schools, human resources, mental health teams or help agencies. No wonder the subject of bullying is so often brushed under the carpet. Yet knowledge gives choice of action, prevention and empowerment. It reduces stress and improves the quality of life. It is spreads understanding, improving communities.

Unlike many books on bullying I cover a broad spectrum; family abuse, school, workplace, community and cyber-bullying. This is for three reasons. First, victims are likely to be victims in several environments. Secondly, each environment has its peculiarities and needs different approaches. Finally, people being bullied and helpers need help fast. They have little energy to read tomes but want rapid access to information, to make informed choices. I want this book to offer knowledge, empowerment and survival for any bully situation.

* * *

LEVEL 1: EMPOWERMENT – SELF CARE, RECORD, REPORT

1: TAKING CARE OF YOURSELF

- prepare for action
- an example of bullying at work
- become assertive by determining to act
- why you need professional support
- never give up skills and talents
- keep a personal journal or diary
- don't let negative feelings fester
- USEFUL ACTION
- remind yourself the bully needs help
- dissipation of adrenaline

Prepare for Action

Whilst each bully environment (home, school, workplace, community) has slightly different requirements, in all cases you need to look after and protect yourself. I assume you are reading this because you are, or have been bullied, or trying to help a victim. Once support is in place, you can tackle the bullying, first reporting then making a record of every incident. **The worst thing to do is nothing**. 'Head in the sand' is a common attitude, in the belief the bullying will stop by itself. All it does is give bullies a false sense of power. Another error is refusing help, telling a would-be helper there is no problem. This is shifting responsibility onto their shoulders and they will be frustrated, guilty or angry at such denial. Will they offer again? Would you?

Put care in place, get support, report and record. These are the first actions for all bullying.

BECOMING ASSERTIVE BY DETERMINING TO ACT

When you act, you begin changes that build confidence over time. You must re-learn trust, a trust you probably lost. Remember, the bully wants to separate you from the qualities that make you, you; skills, talents, decent friends, good reputation, supportive family etc. They want you to feel as lacking and isolated as they do.

Do not worry if anyone, even family, religious leaders or therapists, remark that victims become bullies or that you should forgive. It may be true but during bullying is NOT the right time for worthy action. You need to be indignant, assertive, even angry to gain energy to deal with the situation. Worry about being nice after recovery. Sure, your tendency might be to get over-angry and go further than intended as you 'find your voice'. Being ok around a bully, speaking civilly then making it clear you do not want their presence WILL happen, but not at once. If they show no respect, forgiving them will make you seem weak in their eyes and they will continue bullying, if not you then someone else. I dealt with a workplace pest by shoving her across a corridor when she tried it on once too often. Another I frog-marched from a radio studio after she tried to disrupt my programme. It might not be 'Christian', which is what un-streetwise folk said, but if you ask if this happened to them, family or a friend, the answer is embarrassed silence. It is easy to give advice if you have no experience. Lives are ruined, victims isolated and lose confidence. I still believe, years down the line, I acted rightly. Sometimes you must make a stand as long as you do not break the law! If the bully seeks reform, then is the time to forgive, a gift they must **earn**.

Why You Need Professional Support

I've covered this further in the next section, but get professional support too. Bullying triggers strong emotions which go on to affect physical health – disturbed sleep, anger or crying jags, increased thoughts of revenge, reduced libido, over-thinking, sleeplessness, poor decision-making, bad memory, no concentration, hopelessness and even suicidal thoughts. Bullying triggers bad habits; over-eating, drinking, smoking, gambling, promiscuity, drug-taking. Research shows severe bullying can take up to 10 years to fully recover. A professional is there to listen and point the way to support services. They are non-critical, non-judgemental and confidential. The only time they are obliged to reveal what is said, is if they believe a client will self harm or harm others. After good therapy you will feel relief and learn more about yourself. Often bullying brings back memories of prior abuse or situations never dealt with. This is emotionally difficult but ultimately healing. You will be a stronger person after therapy.

Never Give Up Skills & Talents

Bullies want to separate you from things you love and are good at, the things they envy. **DON'T LET BULLIES WIN BY GIVING UP YOUR SKILLS**. Keep this message on your phone. Never stop doing things you enjoy even if you have little energy. Find a creative mate or mentor who will encourage when you flag. If you don't feel like doing a class, sporting or social event, aim to go and watch. Odds on when you get there you will re-find enthusiasm. There is nothing more soul-destroying than wishing you had gone out when it is too late.

Keep a Personal Journal or Diary

Keep a journal or diary. This is not the same as recording

evidence but helps you cope. Write fears and anxieties, hopes and dreams. Write out anger and frustration and what didn't work. Most importantly, highlight with a marker pen what DID work and what you are learning. This too will empower. If there is something bad to record, aim to add something good to counterbalance. It does not have to be pages; write in bullet points, note form or as if it were a story. Who knows, you might decide you like writing and become an author, blogger or journalist. But this diary is NOT for sharing. When the bullying is over, re-read it and see how much you have changed. Then decide whether or not to keep it. If you decide not to, make a ceremony; burn or throw it in the sea page by page or bury the pages. This is a symbolic 'letting go'.

Don't Let Negative Feelings Fester
Don't let negative feelings fester. Join a boxing club, karate/judo dojo, go running, drive somewhere quiet and scream – then go home and do something life enhancing. Do not let bullying become a lifestyle.

USEFUL ACTIONS:
➢ **Get professional help if your mood is affected**
➢ record, record, record – cctv, audio, notes, find willing witnesses
➢ report threats and violence to police – they keep a record
➢ if you are taunted, wear soft ear plugs /a Walkman **but not near roads**
➢ write to your GP about your mental health – useful for Tribunal
➢ DO NOT HIDE AWAY
➢ use anger to drive your actions; do not let anger fester
➢ maintain friendships and support networks

- ➢ if necessary move to a nicer school or neighbourhood
- ➢ make plans as soon as things get difficult
- ➢ do not 'play into' the victim role – do something, anything
- ➢ discover what the bully hates about you; if a skill, practice more
- ➢ do not join-in by taking revenge or taunting the bully
- ➢ join/start an anti bullying campaign
- ➢ find an anti-bully support group
- ➢ keep up your physical health – walk, sport, gym, meditation
- ➢ continue hobbies & interests
- ➢ don't look back with regret; don't let it destroy you
- ➢ be determined to move on and up
- ➢ don't take up old habits – learn from the past

Remind Yourself, The Bully Needs Help
After a bad day, remind yourself the bully is the wrong doer, not you; fixing their problem is **not** your responsibility. Pat yourself on the back that you have taken the adult decision to empower yourself. The recalcitrant 'old ma' and her delinquent family, the thug who perceives himself as a Robert Mugabe, the 8 year old criminal are not worthy of your respect. Anyone refuses mediation is suspect. Bullies are cowards, too idle to grow talents and skills because they are fearful of risking failure. By all means move school or house to get away from thuggish families or cliques – there is no shame in this, in fact it is wise. Love yourself and know you can start again. They will not have the faculty to do this. Look at those stuck for years in the same neighbourhood who grumble about everything and everyone, but do nothing, go nowhere – just moan.

Dissipation of Adrenaline
Adrenaline, the hormone which causes stress symptoms, reduces naturally after 20 minutes (refer diagrams, adrenaline/

dissipation). I explain this later. This means the physical sensations associated with fear disappear regardless of what you do. Bullies expect victims to remain victims- i.e. doing nothing about it. Whilst it is not sensible to face-off an aggressive bully or gang, staying in anxiety-provoking situations is confidence building and will surprise your bully. If you act appropriately they will back off [*but in the case of sociopaths DO NOT PROVOKE THEM. explained later in the text*].

* * *

SPACE FOR YOUR NOTES:

2: MANAGING EMOTIONS

- Choosing a therapist
- Danger of persistent low mood

There is little free counselling these days. The most common services on offer are public stress management courses. These teach participants about the links between thinking, feeling and action, based on cognitive behavioural therapy (refer Level 3). You might be offered a batch of six Counselling sessions through a GP surgery. If bullying seriously impacts your mental health, your GP can request special funding from the local health commissioners for private psychotherapy. This needs considerable support from your GP, due to demands on funding.

Choosing a Therapist
Though it is best to find a qualified therapist it is often difficult to know what the qualifications mean. There used to be rivalry between private therapy and the NHS but this is less so. Brief therapies are often in line with client's beliefs, more so than medical models and medication. It is better to seek someone you feel comfortable with rather than someone with many qualifications. If there is no one you can ask to recommend a therapist, instinct will guide you to the right person. Thankfully, there is less stigma about revealing we have been in therapy so you are more likely to find someone willing to give you the name of their therapist.

Danger of Persistent Low Mood
If you have, or notice in someone else, enduring out-of-character low mood, it is vital to get immediate professional help. Without wanting to cause alarm, people commit suicide under the

influence of pervasive irrational thoughts. Changes in mood are triggered by bullying and during these times individuals have no insight into the fact they are becoming depressed. Depression is often triggered by life events. It is treatable but requires professional input. A peer, colleague, friend or family member will notice changes in behaviour which point to depression. Depression can also be triggered by trauma, stress, grief, loss, change (good or bad), adolescence, mid- life or onset of old age. Some individuals have a genetic tendency to depression but this is less common. Depression affects 1 in 5 of the population.

* * *

SPACE FOR YOUR NOTES:

3: PROFESSIONAL SUPPORT

- Talking cures
- Cognitive Behavioural Therapy (CBT)

TALKING CURES

Counselling is effective for releasing tension by talking through your problems. A patient of Sigmund Freud coined the term 'talking cure' and it stuck. If anyone you know is experiencing persistent low or high mood, has erratic thoughts or thoughts of self- harm or attacking someone, they need medical attention. A psychiatrist is a doctor qualified in prescribing medication which relieves mental symptoms. There is no shame in being referred to a psychiatrist. Counselling, meditation, mindfulness and cognitive behavioural therapy (CBT) are effective in reducing anxiety and moderate depression.

Cognitive Behavioural Therapy (CBT)

Cognitive Behavioural Therapy (CBT) is based on Stoic philosophy (described in section 4). CBT is based on links between thinking, feeling and behaving. Changing one affects the other two. This is the 'triangle of insight' (see diagram). This is how it works: Primitive man was not consciously aware (aware of his own thinking) but relied on reactions to gut feelings:

1. **trigger** – perceives potential prey, predator or mate (**perceive/think**)
2. **feeling** – gut feeling (**instinct**)
3. **action** – how we react (**behaviour**)

This is quite a difficult concept, so study the diagram then do this exercise. Think of a situation which triggered anxiety (1). What was your gut feeling about it (2)? How did you react as a result (3)? We now know there are gaps of time (pauses) between 1 and 2 (perceiving and feeling) and between 2. & 3 (feeling and acting):

1. we perceive a trigger
   gap of time – we compare this with 'what happened before'
2. as a result, we experience a feeling
   [**gap of time**] perhaps nervously, we decide if it is appropriate to act the same as we did before, or do something different
3. we choose what to do – and experience a benefit

Try the first exercise again but this time use the gaps of time to imagine alternative, positive behaviour. After the mental exercise put this to practice in a bully situation. Keep notes of progress.

* * *

SPACE FOR YOUR NOTES:

Diagram 1: TRIANGLE OF INSIGHT
how thoughts, feelings & behaviour are linked

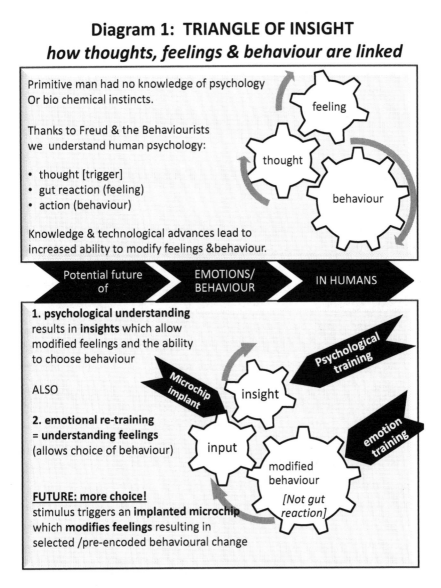

Primitive man had no knowledge of psychology
Or bio chemical instincts.

Thanks to Freud & the Behaviourists
we understand human psychology:

- thought [trigger]
- gut reaction (feeling)
- action (behaviour)

Knowledge & technological advances lead to
increased ability to modify feelings &behaviour.

feeling

thought

behaviour

Potential future of

EMOTIONS/ BEHAVIOUR

IN HUMANS

1. **psychological understanding**
results in **insights** which allow
modified feelings and the ability
to choose behaviour

ALSO

2. **emotional re-training**
= **understanding feelings**
(allows choice of behaviour)

Psychological training

Microchip implant

insight

emotion training

input

modified behaviour
[Not gut reaction]

<u>FUTURE: more choice!</u>
stimulus triggers an **implanted microchip**
which **modifies feelings** resulting in
selected /pre-encoded behavioural change

4: OTHER SELF HELP

- Stoic philosophy
- Quaker Meeting
- mindfulness meditation
- guided meditation
- deep, slow breathing
- re-breathing technique
- deep exhaling
- peer support
- self help groups & books

Stoic Philosophy

Epictetus, Marcus Aurelius and Seneca were philosophers in Ancient Rome of the Stoic school. They encouraged pupils to think before acting; not as others or their emotions dictated. They acknowledged our inclination to 'do as we've always done.' Marcus Aurelius, Emperor of Rome, knew he would be faced by naysayers, sycophants, greedy people and liars. It would be easy to get angry or dismiss them. The great Emperor used Stoicism so he did not shatter his peace by getting angry with difficult people. Epictetus meditated on loss whenever he saw a loved one, thus bracing himself against the knowledge they would one day die. Buddhist religion counsels followers to meditate on death, enhancing every day through gratefulness for being alive.

If you would like to try stoicism, buy, 'The Daily Stoic Journal' and 'The Daily Stoic,' by Ryan Holliday. The first is a blank journal where you can write notes, the second an explanatory book arranged into 365 short extracts from Stoic philosophy with modern interpretations. This is from week XVI:

> The week's theme is impulse control. Ryan offers quotations from Marcus Aurelius followed by a modern explanation. The theme is, 'why are you a slave to your thoughts? Are you a

puppet? Has age taught you nothing about being enslaved in this way?'
Day 2 asks, 'can I stop feeling hurt by every little thing?' What I wrote for day 2 is, 'I am famous for this. I'll make a competition with myself; if X says something rude this week, I'll choose to smile or ignore it.'

Quaker Meetings

The Quakers (Religious Society of Friends) have twice weekly meetings for worship which anyone can attend. They are midweek with a longer one hour on Sunday, followed by coffee and chat. Do not be put off by the word, 'worship'. Many spiritual people do not accept the existence of a God but, like Quakers, follow a spiritual (moral) path. The Quaker precept is, 'go lightly through the world seeing that of good in everyone.' Quakers do not have hymns, readings or prayers but anyone who feels moved can speak during the silence. Weddings and funerals are conducted in similar fashion. Emotionally uplifting, these celebrations of life move Attenders to laughter or tears at anecdotes about the departed or married couple. The experience of being with others in a spiritual setting, whilst not obliged to communicate works well for anyone with autism, those who lack social confidence or are challenged by social situations.

Mindfulness Meditation

Mindfulness was developed by Buddhist monks for meditation practice during everyday activity. It became popular in the West as a treatment for mild to moderate depressive illness instead of medication. For this purpose, mindfulness has been approved by NICE (National Institute for Clinical Excellence). The first, and best, book on the subject is The Miracle of Mindfulness by Thitch Nath Hanh, the Buddhist monk who brought the practice to the West. Mindfulness appears simple yet needs practice. It is about living in the moment on whatever you are doing, be it gardening, washing dishes or sweeping the floor. This is something we think we do but rarely do properly. This is an example. Pick up a household object and look at it carefully. Is it hard or soft, warm or cold? Can you see light along its edges or detect ripples on its surface? What colour is it? Do changes of light alter its features? Does it bring memories? Try this method whilst eating an orange. Do you taste each segment or are you doing something else whilst eating? When you attempt this meditation, the most humble act is endowed with discovery. We go about our lives thinking of the past and worrying about the future. Rarely do we live in the moment. The present moment lasts eight seconds! How much time do we spend worrying about things we cannot change or agonizing over what has gone or what is to be? Try to live mindfully.

Guided Meditation

Guided meditation can be practised alone or in a group. If alone, there are tapes and CD's available where a therapist talks you through a scenario – an imaginary walk through woods or by a lake. Other guided meditation focuses on parts of the body, in turn tensing then relaxing muscles until the body is relaxed. Guided meditation can be with or without music.

Deep, Slow Breathing

Deep, slow breathing relaxes mind and body, resulting in calm and well being. The practice can be done anywhere but outdoors gives an even more pleasant effect. This method has been used for thousands of years as yoga practice, long before we knew how and why it worked. Beginners will find it useful to join a class. Most Buddhist centres offer free or with a small donation meditation classes in larger towns. Formal classes are listed on the Internet and in libraries (*if you are lucky enough to have one*).

Re-Breathing Technique, for Anxiety and Panic

Re-breathing using a brown paper bag (**never plastic**) is a rapid way of recovering from hyperventilation (panic attack). Put the paper bag over your mouth (not your nose) then breath slowly in and out. During panic attacks, the tendency is to breathe too rapidly which sends too much oxygen into the blood. Re-breathing carbon dioxide allows your body to recover more quickly than using deep, slow breathing.

Deep Exhaling

Breathing out longer than you breathe in is calming and reduces anxiety symptoms. This is easier to achieve if you count as you breathe – breathe in through the nose for a count of 7 then breathe out through the mouth for a count of 11. Focusing on counting takes the mind away from the physical symptoms.

Psychologists quantified many ancient spiritual practises into therapeutic relief for emotional problems. These practises are easily available through books, often free at Buddhist centres or Wellbeing Colleges run by Local Authorities.

Peer Support

A useful way of sharing experiences is to find a group of pupils, workmates or tenants who are or have been bullied and organise an informal meeting to share experiences, ideas and swap contacts, then have a social. This used to be called co-counselling. Meet in a youth club, hire a room in a library or business centre, each other's homes (if you know the others well enough) on a rotation basis or if age-appropriate a pub, club or online. In the latter case, beware trolling and restrict the group to members only. It is better to have an agenda and a formal meeting then allow time to relax. Limit the time each person speaks to allow the maximum number to talk if they wish. Attending a peer group is empowering, more so than talking to family or friends who have not experienced bullying.

There are plenty of anti-bullying websites which offer peer support. The international ones are 24 hours, 7 days a week so when you get home from a toxic environment there is someone available to chat, a place to leave a message or accessible information. The Tim Field Foundation website (see resources) has excellent information.

Self Help Groups & Books
There are many self-help books and tapes. You can buy these books second-hand very cheaply from Amazon or ABE Books. There are books on every anxiety and fear. It is comforting to consider how huge the market is; this proves how common anxiety is, which makes it less isolating. I believe novels and films are equally as empowering as non fiction or biography. Fiction might be 'made up' but authors base books on common human experience. There is a range of material in the Resources section. Empowerment is not only action but learning about yourself from a wide range of resources. Bullying is common world wide, so there is no lack of material.

In the 21st century, huge strides have been taken to reduce the effect of bullying. Refer to, 'Bullying in the Community,' where I describe the 2017 updates to 2014 Anti-Social Behaviour Crime & Policing Act which is now wide ranging, often dealing on the spot with bully behaviour. Many resources are spent on research to inform treatment, publications and public services. Taking interest in new anti-bullying measures and doing what you can to redress bullying is also empowering.

* * *

SPACE FOR YOUR NOTES:

5: RECORD AND REPORT CRIMINAL BULLYING

- why you must report bullying
- why you need to record bullying
- keeping records
- police
- Housing Association
- Local Authority
- about Community Trigger

Why You Must Report Bullying

ALWAYS report bullying, even if you fear consequences. Except for police, who have to act when given evidence, you can ask whoever you are reporting to, you want no action at present. However, by doing so you are ham-stringing that person or organisation. You will find relief when you have taken action. You may feel your heart pound but as Dr Susan Jeffers said, 'feel the fear and do it anyway.' If the bully is physically violent, has weapons or a gang, you MUST report this to the police. Not reporting puts you and others in MORE danger. Once your report is on record you should get a more rapid response from police community support officers.

Every report is filed and becomes part of evidence, for future court cases. Whether or not you report will not change a bully's character BUT might prevent tragedy for someone else, if not you. The police know the bad characters in their patch from intelligence (information) provided by the public. Bullies who bluster and threaten 'if you do xx, I'll get you,' are likely 'all mouth and trousers.' A violent bully acts not threatens. If you FEEL threatened even if no one has harmed you, if someone has thrown stones or damaged property, report it. Threatening behaviour is a criminal act.

There are many help organisations for victims of aggressive

bullying and hate crime, accessed via the police; Victim support, Lighthouse, Community Trigger, Sari (see Resources). These agencies offer counselling, checkups and support. If things get bad, police and some Housing Associations have wellbeing houses where you can rest for up to a week. Do not be embarrassed to ask. I have been to one, and it was beneficial.

Why You Need to Record Bullying

At the same time as reporting, it is vital to record all incidents of bully behaviour (refer following section). First you need evidence in case bullying escalates to criminal acts. The Crown Prosecution Service (CPS) looks at police evidence to decide whether or not to prosecute. Second, once you start recording, the bully's behaviour patterns become clear. For example, you might notice bullying occurs more often at a particular time or day of the week. You might notice they use certain words or phrases or react to 'trigger words' (words or phrases which annoy, escalate or calm the situation). All this is useful learning to deal with your bully. Third, writing things down answers questions like, 'why me?'. In recovery (*which happens sporadically, increasing in duration and length*) you can analyse what you noticed and this too is empowering. It is something you can discuss with a therapist or friend or mentor.

On the road to recovery it is empowering to see how far you have travelled but without records you will not remember. With a record, things that seemed hopeless will show your progress. The road to recovery is never smooth but by recording you continue to fight back.

There are civil laws dealing with written (defamatory) or verbal (libellous) abuse. Taking someone to court is expensive unless you find a pro bono (goodwill) barrister. But if the abuse is hate crime, a prosecution under criminal law is likely.

Keeping Records

When you make a log, CCTV or audio recording, keep it secure. Don't let anyone have access, even loved ones. You do not want evidence leaking by accident. Imagine this: People get angry on your behalf and in the throes of emotion innocently reveal what you have written. People offer opinions, and opinions cannot be allowed to contaminate evidence. Confidentiality gives evidence special status, separating it from daily life. If you want to write about the agonies, do that in a journal.

So what do the police or help agencies need to know? Think of writer Rudyard Kipling and his six serving men: who, what, when, where, how and why. If there are witnesses, ask if they are prepared to give a report. Be prepared for disappointment. It is common for people to fear being involved. Courts are stressful, with hectoring Barristers who do not consider witness feelings. It is not something everyone can face. If you get a witness report, hand originals to the police and keep a copy; you can also report incidents online, which is confidential and does not get attached to email. This is a sample personal recording log:

> Sat 18th June 2.40 am woken by noise inside front gate. Heard someone fiddling front door lock with bunch of keys and attempting to open door. Got up and shouted. Saw youth running off. Grey hoodie, red mud on trainers and back of blue trousers. Slim build, hood over head.

> Sunday 19th 3:40am had padlocked gate. padlock being fiddled with. Pulled blinds and a few seconds later headlights of a vehicle parked opposite my window switched on. Two men inside, white teenagers. One same build as yesterday. Face familiar? Passenger shouted then spat at my gate as they drove past. Driver sleeked, gelled black hair, short goatee. Van medium sized, whitish, dirty, scratch on rear panel.

Tues 21st gate open, back door open with bolts off, door glass broken. Plant pot next to door broken. Nothing missing. Small smear of blood on broken glass – took swab with cotton bud. Fri 24th rock thrown at front window bounced and landed on grass. Saw youth running off – red T shirt, black shorts, dirty trainers.

Other useful devices are digital audio recording devices, CCTV or webcams. You cannot direct CCTV's onto neighbouring property or a highway only in the perimeter of your property. Audio recording must be sited on your property. Rough sketches of the vicinity are useful with features such as windows, fences, bus shelters, direction of travel or public CCTV. It is easier to interpret events from a diagram than description.

Below are the major agencies, how to report incidents and type of bullying dealt with. There is overlap but the agencies information-share, where allowable by law.

POLICE

The police deal with serious anti-social behaviour (ASB). More often than not this is handled by support officers whose job it is to ensure residents enjoy the peace and security of home without being subjected to harassment, criminal damage or intimidation. 999 is for emergencies, injury, danger from vehicles, environmental danger or if miscreants are in the vicinity. For non emergencies use 101. The police have 7 day / 24 hour call centres. The following are dealt with by community police:

- verbal abuse and threats
- serious littering i.e. dumping on private property
- excess noise, drunkenness, drug-taking
- behaviour likely to cause alarm to residents (breach of peace)
- domestic violence

- hate crime – verbal / physical abuse directed at racial origin, gender, disability, sexual orientation or religious belief
- stalking – following someone with intent to frighten or harm
- criminal damage to property
- cyber-bullying – written abuse via the Internet
- sexting – sending offensive text and/or images of a sexual nature
- grooming – older men contacting minors of either sex, with the aim of sex

HOUSING ASSOCIATION
Tenants can report bully behaviours to a landlord:

- littering / fouling property or vicinity of victim
- sending hate mail [inform police]
- damage to property [inform police]
- using offensive language, catcalling, racial abuse [inform police]
- shouting, door-slamming, excess noise after midnight [inform council]
- inciting neighbours to abuse victim [inform police]
- interfering with right of tenant to live peacefully in their home

LOCAL AUTHORITY
- excessive noise nuisance [inform Local Authority or Housing Association]
- littering or fouling of victim's property

The Local Authority will fit recording devices in your home if the noise is persistent. If it is a rowdy party they can confiscate the offender's audio equipment. Refer to the section on bullying in the Community, which describes in detail new Police Act and powers delegated to Housing Associations and Local Authorities.

SPACE FOR YOUR NOTES:

6: RECORD & REPORT NON CRIMINAL BULLYING

- bullying: criminal & anti-social behaviour (ASB)
- examples of anti-social behaviour

Bullying: Criminal & anti-social behaviour

To repeat, bullying is behaviour designed to humiliate and demean the target. It can be expressed through violence but more often it is psychological; taunting, damaging, hiding property, sexual shaming, cyber-bullying, spreading malicious gossip or lying about the victim to isolate them. Certain classes of bullying are criminalised as in Hate Crime. The following list contains examples of bullying and where to report it.

Anti-social behaviours:

- littering – housing association or local authority
- noise nuisance – local authority
- name calling – if hate crime, report to police
- pushing substances through letterbox – see criminal bullying
- nuisance in social housing – anti-social behaviour team
- taunting [at school] – head, teacher, assistant, counsellor, parent
- cyber bullying – report to service provider, school and ISP of the bully
- sexual shaming or sexting – head teacher. see criminal bullying.
- damage or theft to property (any environment) – see criminal bullying
- lesser damage e.g. egg throwing – usually schools, report as above
- tripping up victim – schools, report to teacher
- physical violence – see criminal bullying
- hiding property / work – schools, workplace; report to teacher,

HR, spreading malicious gossip – anti bullying ambassador, counsellor
- telling lies to get victim in trouble – teacher, HR
- excluding victim from socials or ignoring their contribution – teacher, head, school counsellor; workplace HR or EAP

This list is not exhaustive. Bullies are repetitive so knowing what to do is empowering. Do you see how petty some of these behaviours are? Tripping; hiding a bag or piece of clothing, spreading gossip; throwing litter; ringing a doorbell then running away. The more mean the act, the more desperate the bully. A bully has low self-esteem and is trying to drag the victim down. Think of this every time they anger, annoy or frighten you.

The source of your power lies in realising what your bully is targeting. Rather than concentrating on how they behave, try analysing WHY they are targeting you, then use it for your own self improvement.

* * *

SPACE FOR YOUR NOTES:

7: BULLYING IN SCHOOLS

- who bullies whom
- likely victims
- where bullying is likely to take place
- types of bullying in schools
- teacher behaviour in the 1950's
- alternatives

- STRATEGIES FOR THE VICTIM
- WHAT NOT TO DO
- ACTION BY STAFF
- ACTION BY PARENTS & HELPERS
- COMMENT

Who Bullies Whom

Bullying in schools is an imbalance of power, often teacher on pupil but can be the other way around. Gang on individual, gang on gang or individual to individual, if behaviour demeans, humiliates or hurts intentionally, this is classed as bullying. Gone are the days when teachers wielded canes, hurled blackboard erasers or twisted young ears to hive off frustration at pupil behaviour (*or problems in their personal lives*). It is harder to prove emotional abuse where abusers uses subtle ways of cutting a victim down. Being on the end of abusive behaviour can (*but does not always*) lead to victims becoming bullies in later life; domestic abuse, anti-social behaviour or criminal activity, and so down the generations. Hurts can be remembered a long time. Read the poem, 'This Be the Verse' by Philip Larkin.

Many a teacher lost a career to bullying, provoked or not, but this does not redress the hurt of victims. On the other side, many a teacher has unfairly lost a job to false claims of abuse or sexual abuse by pupils. Sensitive teachers have a hard time from aggressive pupils who manipulate known weaknesses.

Thankfully, personality-disordered bullies are rarer than chancers, the frustrated person who lacks confidence but might, with help, turn their life around. Newbies are often first to be targeted. Innocent newcomers do not 'play the game' by showing deference to self-elected leaders. They have not yet worked out who to trust and may have insufficient know-how to do so. A school with decent anti-bully ambassadors is the best place for individuals likely to become victims.

Likely Victims
There is no single profile for a victim. It is not weakness of character, a frequent and unnecessary shame for victims. If there is something good, decent or worthy about you, that can mark you out for bullying. If you are talented, skilled, a good communicator, fashionable, good looking – that marks you out. Bullying is mainly about envy and lack of self-esteem. **Hold onto that thought.**

There are broad strokes that separate likely-to-be-targeted individuals from others. Bullies are useful in that they inadvertently help you discover skills and talents, if you can get under the radar of victim-hood. It is your task to find out what it is they fear or envy about you, then to develop that trait. I will keep repeating this very valuable lesson.

Here are some useful facts. Incomers are likely victims, particularly if markedly different to existing pupils. Those of different race, creed, physical appearance, disability, intellectual level (lower or higher). Also vulnerable are individuals who wear shabby or dirty clothing, clothes perceived unfashionable, glasses or hearing aids. Strangely, some disabilities now have an aura of 'glamour' and those 'supporting' them given high status; for example a bully might blanch at attacking a wheelchair-bound pupil; 'I choose to help this person' or 'I protect them.' Yet seeing a nervous, spotty child, crack-toothed with glasses, the bully will hound them. Why? It makes their little minds feel better – i.e. they think they are 'one up' on a defenceless person.

Others likely to stand out for persecution are creatives; those who prefer study to rough-and-tumble, generate ideas unacceptable to the group or wear outlandish clothes. *'They are so different they are asking for it'*, thinks the bully. Lastly, anyone more popular than the bully or their cronies, individuals perceived as rivals, anyone with outstanding looks, attractive personality, high intellect or gifted.

Where Bullying is Likely to Take Place

Bullying more often happens where there are no overseers patrolling in breaks and lunchtime. So, victims need to seek places where there are people – like a library, canteen or playground. Many schools have pre and after school clubs; other potential refuges. Do not be afraid to go and ask for help if you are being harried. Better feel a bit of embarrassment than be hurt. Outside school gates is a recognised danger zone. Pupils have been attacked for petty things like wearing the 'wrong' uniform, appearance or lack of fashion sense. Outside school gates is often perceived no man's land, but the new Police Act gives teachers powers to deal with incidents out of school too. This must have been in part due to brave Headmaster Philip Lawrence who died protecting a pupil from a knife-wielding bully outside his school gates.

Types of Bullying in Schools

Often, victims are unsure if they are being bullied because some behaviours appear petty on the surface. The key is **expectation** and **repetition**. If someone demeans you over a long period of time, this is bullying.

Here are some examples:

- swearing, offensive or personal remarks (taunting)
- offensive remarks about race, disability, gender identity, appearance
- intimidation – pushing, shoving, verbal threats
- physical attacks, threats of violence with or without weapons
- cruel remarks about appearance, clothing, smells
- hiding property – school bags, homework, clothing
- stalking [following or encouraging others to follow the victim]
- damage to victim's property
- inciting others to humiliate or taunt
- sexual shaming
- cyber bullying
- bait out
- ridicule
- ignoring or sidelining victim's contribution to class work
- derailing the victim's work
- psychological abuse – taunting, name-calling, spreading gossip or lies
- emotional abuse – menacing
- cyber-bullying – spreading rumours by email, phone, on the internet
- isolating e.g. victimising, spreading gossip, shaming, negating target's values, skills, talents, ignoring (stone walling)
- getting target in trouble by manipulating or lying

Teacher Behaviour in the 1950's
Bullying has only recently been recognised as damaging. After the war corporal punishment in schools was approved of, harking back to earlier times: soldiers who became teachers on returning from horrific experiences in the First or Second World Wars expected boys to act tough and girls to be biddable. The idea of punishment to 'toughen up' youngsters makes some

sense in that historical context. A side-line was intolerance of quiet kids; intellectuals, creatives, those with artistic or musical ability, individuals who abhor violence. Watch the film, 'Billy Elliott' and try to understand the attitude of the Northern father who mocks his son for wanting to be a ballet dancer. Acceptable behaviour in those times is now socially unacceptable; slapping, strapping, caning, hurling wooden blackboard erasers, twisting ears. Another punishment was sending pupils to stand in a corner, their back to the wall, sometimes wearing a tall, pointed paper hat with 'Dunce' written on it. Sound primitive? To us yes; to pupils and teachers of the time it was accepted.

Pupils at public schools endured worse with fagging (acting as servant to older boys), beatings, cold baths and even homosexual rape. It is now believed caning and such-like were not just corporal punishments but a covert form of sexual deviancy. Corporal punishment was banned in state schools in 1986 and 1998 in private schools. This did not mean bullying by teachers died out. It took on the form of psychological abuse; verbal abuse, put downs, singling pupils for ridicule and encouraging others to do the same. Other damaging behaviour by teachers is spoiling or downgrading assignments which can seriously damage future careers.

The most gross type of teacher behaviour is sexual abuse of boys and girls. Sexual abuse of a minor and grooming are serious criminal offences and must be reported to the police. No one condemns victims who 'come out' and help convict an offender. There are cases where precocious pupils seduce a teacher but in law the teacher is deemed liable.

Alternatives

While it is never pleasant to consider moving school, this is doubly awkward if it necessitates moving house. If you decide to remain, you must adapt. Don't expect the bully to change because 99% will not. Perhaps the school provides specialist training or is the only one in commuting distance. It might have things that are too good to lose. If this is the case, the victim must be taught to deal with the bully – to avoid or control them using psychology (refer to Triangle of insight).

If you decide moving is best, make sure the new school is informed of the bullying. Also, check out their anti bullying measures. Schools are required to have measures by law but it is best to check what exactly is in place. If your child or a relative is gifted or has a sporting bent, they might thrive in a public or grammar school. Many have bursaries which cover fees so do not be ashamed to ask.

STRATEGIES FOR THE VICTIM
The best exit is moving towards what Carl Jung called individuation; discovery of the true self. Do what bullied celebrities (see Resources) did – discover your passion and develop it. Diving deep into any subject helps psychologically shut out bullying. Take professional advice on how to handle a bully. This means detached observation. Find out what triggers their rage, laughter, suspicion, what makes them stop. So long as your bully is not a sociopath or narcissist, a tip from Stella O'Malley's book, Bully Proof Kids; say firmly but clearly, 'you need help,' before walking away. Bullies are not flexible and find it hard to respond to unexpected behaviour. Another tactic is to say hello and continue walking as if they have not bothered you. Do not smile or the bully will think you are laughing at them. Remember, never return insults or catcalls. Carry audio recording equipment, but well hidden. Continue to record all incidents.

Do Not Hope the Bully Will Go Away

Doing nothing is not a good idea. Over time everything degenerates, a factor known as entropy. Entropy exists in human behaviour. There are decent people and (sadly) there are wicked people.

One of the great artists- poets William Blake wrote;

'man was born for joy and woe
and when this we truly know
Safely through the world we go.'

It is understandable why people remain in denial. We like to think of our fellow men as nice, understanding. We want to believe if we show them we are nice too they will leave us alone. This is white (or blue-sky) thinking (refer diagram, Perceptions). Or, if we explain ourselves, we hope a bully will understand and reciprocate. This rarely works. Some are motivated to change after wasting many years in prison or solitary confinement. Some never change.

On a positive note, the seemingly impossible does happen. Read, 'The Bird Man of Alcatraz' by Thomas E Gaddis *(on which the film of the same name was based)*. This tells the true story of psychopath Robert Stroud. After committing murder, Stroud spent 54 of 73 years in prison, 42 in solitary confinement. During his sentence he began raising canaries, becoming an expert in avian disease and setting up a business selling birds. This ended when he was moved to Alcatraz. Though a violent prisoner disliked by peers and guards alike, Stroud found peace using his high intellect to study ornithology, later studying law and French. Stroud's story is considered a success by penal reformists; not that his personality disorder was cured but how he learned to cope, becoming a model prisoner. Over the years many ornithologists pleaded for his release but Stroud died in prison.

Sociopaths, Narcissists and Violent Bullies

The most dangerous type of bully is the sociopath. Smiling and confident, often popular and just as likely to target those in authority as victims they perceive to be weak. Note, I said PERCEIVE weak. Victims are not weak but 90% of people would weaken under the relentless targeting of a sociopath. Sociopaths and Narcissists are hard to detect until their mask is broken, usually by a hit on their pride or failure to comply with demands, which unleashes a torrent of revenge. If you suspect your bully has a personality disorder (see Major Players) DO NOT confront them. Sociopaths and narcissists need careful handling, best left to experts. On first meeting they will try to discover how biddable you are and try to gather information which will be used against you. For kids, the best thing to do is acknowledge them (*they hate being ignored*) then walk off as if you have an appointment. They cannot read minds and will not know what you are doing.

Likewise, it is best to avoid bullies who are physically or verbally violent. They are likely to be surrounded by a fawning gang of toadies who see punching, kicking or knife crime as thrilling. They rarely fear authority, going out of their way to defy its representatives. They rise to dares and respond with an attack to perceived insults no matter how trivial. Many bullies have been bullied themselves but this is no excuse for their behaviour, so do not feel sorry for them. Bullying is a choice.

Psychological Bullies

These bullies use well-chosen words to hurt, rather than physical violence. They can be male or female, whereas most physical bullies are male. Record and report all incidents. Perhaps in their childhood they were mocked by parents and as a result gave up. In time, you might find yourself sorry for them, but do not let this prevent you from freeing yourself of them.

BEATING THE BULLY

The Frenemy

A frenemy is an enemy who poses as a friend. They ferret out secrets and reveal them to others, using particularly juicy information to hurt or humiliate. Or they might smile and make a sarcastic 'joke' against you to mutual friends. If you get angry, they feign surprise, making a pretence of hurt so friends turn against you. The behaviour of sociopaths is similar though replacing a hurt look with rage. They reserve frenemy behaviour for a single target from one group, because if they acted badly to everyone the group would reject them. People like them for their colourful gossip, hard to resist when coupled with mocking caricatures of the target. Watch the film, 'Carrie' and you will see what I mean. Not everyone will recognise their behaviour as bullying, so do not be hurt if your friends appear to be joking along with them. Frenemies are deeply damaged individuals, 'getting off' through humiliating others. Be assured, you have done nothing to deserve this shoddy behaviour, so do not blame yourself. It is useful in all cases of frenemies to seek counselling, to help you overcome the hurt of betrayal.

How to deal with them? Many young people do not know how to deal with frenemies. It is no shame to seek advice. If not your parent, find a relative who has time to listen or better still a school counsellor. Tell them your worries, hopes and fears and they will help generate ideas to help, without your losing trust and hope.

There are things you ought not to do with a frenemy. One is be confrontational. They will be good at manipulating and seek revenge if you try to expose them. Never let on they have got under your skin. Save emotional responses for your helper. There is an old saying; if you know you have an enemy it is best to keep them close; but this is only for very strong-minded

36

individuals like Queen Elizabeth I. Your task is to starve them of information. Only tell deep secrets, especially sexual secrets, to friends you have known a long, long time and really trust.

If you have a large group of friends, it might be difficult to exclude a frenemy because some of the group might like them. It is better to distance yourself by not answering their texts or messaging. Add them to your mobile as a contact, then you can see who is calling and ignore the call. if you spot a frenemy at a social, acknoweldge them if they catch your eye then immediately find a friend to talk to. Resist joining a knot of people if the frenemy is with them; mouth 'hi' and move on. Try not to show anger or surprise (think of it as acting a part while they are around). If they come over to chat and you don't want to, fake an appointment. Don't tell them what for, even if they put on fake hurt. Don't make it obvious you are pushing a frenemy out of your life. Pull away slowly. Put new friendships in place before you begin to pull away from the old group.

If the frenemy does 'poison' the group, remember there are billions of people in this world. Dr Samuel Johnson the famous lexicographer said, 'a man must keep his friendships in constant repair.' Friendships ebb and flow as you and they develop. No matter you are feeling bad, join a new club or activity, perhaps something you have never tried. When you find something that appeals, you will discover new friends with similar values (morals). Friendships based on values rather than activity are more likely to last. For example, if you love history, volunteer for an archaeological dig. If you love dancing, take beginner lessons in a different type of dancing. It might seem simple but these things are never obvious when reeling from a breakup with a frenemy.

Remember, you cannot choose family but you CAN choose friends. A large circle of acquaintances, a few close friends and something interesting to do every day is the best antidote to a frenemy – and the road to happiness.

Stand Your Ground

With any type of bully **except sociopaths** make a huge effort to counter their behaviour. Bullies watch your reactions, weighing up your confidence and seeing if you are upset. If early on you make it clear you are going to 'fight back' they are less likely to keep trying. Always give good eye contact. In her excellent book, 'Bully Proof Kids', Stella O'Malley suggests 'the 8 second rule'. Keep firm eye contact with a bully for eight seconds and they will see you mean business. Research has shown it takes 8 seconds to register confidence no matter you are churning inside. Remember fight/flight/freeze? If your adrenaline is up, so is theirs. Fear and fight are both reactions to adrenaline (refer diagram, Adrenaline)! Breathe deeply, ignore your wildly beating heart and tingling fingers and count slowly. If they make verbal threats, keep breathing deeply and continue walking but never respond; do not insult or catcall back. Always walk confidently, no matter how you feel. If they shout, do not run or look back unless they begin to chase you, in which case get to a responsible adult / safe place immediately.

Do not become 'class clown' or laugh at yourself in front of them. This is self defeating and over time will reduce your self esteem. Class clowns are not respected, not even in later life when they become stand-up comedians performing the same trick. Some laugh but many inwardly groan. Confident people do not set themselves up then pull themselves down. Your aim is to retain self esteem.

If the bully begins a verbal rant, protest without shouting or getting emotional. Do not sit and fume. A few well chosen words are enough. Practice at home until you are word perfect. Say why you don't like the behaviour, maintaining eye contact and speaking firmly. Being firm but fair others may come to your aid. When you have said your say, turn and walk away. If they cajole others into insulting you this can be upsetting, even scary. See if there is anyone you can call upon for support, an adult or anti bully ambassador if you are in school. Another trick is to use visualisation. Imagine the sound of their voice being slowly turned down as on a TV or radio. Imagine the colour of their skin and clothing fading. Imagine their voice getting squeaky or babyish – but DO NOT LAUGH. These techniques will distract you from what they are doing and ease the impact of their presence.

Do Not Be Isolated – Find Support.
It is vital to get support quickly. I mean professional counselling either at school or through a GP. This will give you support whilst you learn to deal with the bully. And, of course, you MUST report the bullying and keep records.

You have seen people who witness bullying yet walk away. It is not your fault! These people are called bystanders. There are many reasons for their behaviour which I explain in level 2. Be aware, any bystander is capable of becoming an upstander, someone who might be persuaded to help. Go to a nearby adult, look in their eyes and say you need help because you are being bullied. If they look embarrassed /do not reply /do not give you eye contact, ask someone else. If there is no one around, walk (don't run) to the nearest place with a school-appointed anti bully ambassador or responsible adult (teacher, assistant or anyone who works in your school). When you find someone, ask them to let you stand next to them until the bully goes away, then report what happened. If this adult will go with you all the better. There is no shame in doing this. I've done it and things turned out.

Schools are obliged by law to put anti bullying measures in place so find out what your school does as soon as you can. This often includes anti bully ambassadors appointed from among senior pupils. The school might have a buddy bench where if you sit on it an anti bully ambassador will come over to talk to you. The ambassadors are there for anyone who needs support so do not feel shy about approaching them.

If no adult is around go to a place where there are plenty of people like a playground or a library – anywhere where there are staff. If the bully follows, keep away from areas you are likely to be alone. And never be tempted to leave the premises, because you will be vulnerable.

Keep up friendships and make new ones. Join school clubs and groups before and after school. There is nothing that builds confidence as much as belonging to a group of like-minded individuals. It is likely that many will have experienced bullying but do not to make that the prime reason for attending. If your club ends late at night, make sure a parent or sibling has agreed to take you home. In many attacks the victim is a person who took a risk. Victims are tempted to take risks hoping to 'prove' they are not afraid. It is dangerous to do this.

If you have a condition or disability offer a talk to your class or the whole school. This will not only educate fellow pupils but give you a boost. It is not easy speaking in class but after the first time you will never regret it. It will stand you in good stead for working life.

WHAT NOT TO DO

We covered what not to do in the case of sociopaths and frenemies, but there are certain actions which will annoy bullies and rouse their ire. As with mad cows or bulls, it is better to leave the field than get hurt.

It is important to remain the pleasant person you are. Your friends and teachers will be watching your reactions as well as the bully. You don't want to end up with a bad reputation because you became enraged and the bully took advantage (they are good at provoking then blaming a victim). First, never patronise your bully. Do not use clever remarks, analyse their character, use sarcasm or your intellect to floor them especially if you are more intelligent. The bully will not understand what you are trying to do and will lash out. Bullies are easily aroused emotionally and incapable of self control. Think of them as tyrant toddlers. And never insult them back. It will only escalate matters. If you do hurl insults, outsiders and bystanders will not know who started it and may not offer help when you need it. Stand your ground, be firm but fair and help will often come your way.

ACTION BY STAFF – some ideas
practicalities:
- buddy benches
- anti bullying ambassadors, recruited among mature pupils
- have a worry box – confidential box where kids write /'post' concerns
- offer 1-2-1 with a school counsellor
- allow anonymous reporting [of bullying]
- encourage 'random acts of kindness'
- encourage pupils to record things they are grateful for

Training
- teach anti bullying psychology e.g. to 'box clever'
- mindfulness and meditation training
- diversity awareness
- sociograms – relationships
- cyber safety

Mediation

- try to get a system of restorative justice
- offer peer mediation where appropriate

ACTION BY PARENTS & OTHER HELPERS

Listening

Do the right thing and you can help the victim benefit from the experience of bullying. Listen, listen and listen. Most people do this the other way round; lots of advice (*usually counter-productive*) emotion and a tendency to go steaming to the bully's house. We have two ears and one mouth for a purpose! Do not allow feelings to get in the way of understanding what is going on. It is not good for a child to hold-in emotions. This Victorian thinking can lead to depression, even suicide. Even if you experienced bullying yourself, every situation is different. Let your child reveal as much as they need to allowing plenty of time. There will be ups and downs but all experiences help the child develop, given support and understanding.

Record & Report

If victim moves school, tell the new school what went on. Always record and report incidents. If your child is reluctant, persuade them over time how important it is. If they prefer you to report it, record facts, dates, times. Do not write opinions, anger or whom you blame. Next, persuade the victim to attend counselling; a school counsellor or via a GP. A child will tell an outsider things they keep from you. This is normal so don't feel left out. Find out who the anti bully ambassadors are so you can tell the victim, but do not approach them yourself. Remember, they are chosen as mature individuals but they are not professionals and would be alarmed by approaches from an adult.

If the Bully is a Teacher

If the bully is a teacher, go to the Head and keep doing so while it continues. If the Head fails to act, write to the Governors asking for a written response within a set period. Written requests without a required response date result in delaying or no answer at all;' staff unsure what to do, fearing reprisals or parent suing, use this tactic to evade responsibility.

Using a Go-Between

If you wish, find a go-between between yourself and the Head. This can be a sympathetic teacher, counsellor, form teacher or teaching assistant. If your child has a disability such as autism, individuals who know your child well are a boon. However, do not expect professionals to understand a child's disability or how the child is affected by bullying.

Mediation

Could you, without being emotional, meet the bully's parents? Is it possible or would you prefer a third party to intervene? This depends on how you handle stressful situations. You might be met with denial and counter accusations. How will you deal with this? Practice situations at home before you offer. And take a witness who is independent. Perhaps the school might provide neutral ground and a mediator.

Encourage Victim to Continue Activities

Make sure the victim continues going to clubs and outings. Their tendency might be to get demoralized and give up but this means the bully has won and your child will lose face. Perhaps you can organise someone in the group to meet at the victim's house and go together. When they return, ask what they did, how they enjoyed it and casually discover if the activity is 'doing it' for them.

Look for Signs of Deterioration

Any loss of interest in activity or drop-off in marks for school work might be symptomatic of depression if coupled with low mood. If this happens, get the bullied child to a GP for assessment. Without wishing to alarm, suicide of the victim is a serious risk in bullying situations.

Give Encouragement, Praise & Responsibility

At home give encouragement. Reduce criticism without being over the top. When they tell you about the day, discuss the bullying but encourage them to talk about what went right, what they enjoyed or learnt. Allow them responsibility at home. Can they do some family shopping or take the dog for a walk?

Getting Into the Natural World

If they dislike sport, get them into the natural world, a great healer and teacher. Perhaps outings to nature reserves, walks or lying on a blanket having competitions to name constellations. This sort of thing brings the family closer. Invite friends for picnics and outings. There are many free activities if money is a problem.

Don't Openly Criticise or Gossip About the Bullying

Don't criticise or put down the child to anyone, no matter how they react. It is no one else's business unless they can help the family through the crisis. Many people want gossip to enliven their dull life. Let these sad individuals find other entertainment.

COMMENT

'The only thing necessary for the triumph of evil', 18th century English politician Edmund Burke remarked, 'is that good men do nothing'.

Bullying, especially by kids, should not happen in caring societies. Many agencies believe community spirit has decreased since the Second World War. People lead busy, stressful lives and are often indifferent to other people's difficulties. Where a bully is violent, those brave enough to report crime or appear as witnesses face a struggle; barracking defence lawyers, fear of revenge or censure by rights activists.

Responsibility means not leaving victims fearful and isolated. Why not start a campaign, encourage kids and friends to take part. Take your turn in the witness box if need be. Anti-bully ambassadors and anti bullying training go a long way to redressing toxic environments. As a parent, try to add value. Ask the school if volunteer parents can help cover breaks or patrol quiet areas where bullies are likely to operate? The visibility of parents would send a strong message as well as support time-pressed staff and heads. The Government need to ensure anti bullying measures are in place in every school, sending mystery shoppers with no prior notice where possible.

* * *

SPACE FOR YOUR NOTES:

8: CYBER BULLYING

- who bullies whom
- likely victims
- common signs of cyber bullying
- FORMS OF CYBER BULLYING:
- ACTION FOR VICTIMS:
- ACTION FOR PARENTS/ HELPERS:
- COMMENT

Who Bullies Whom

The Internet is marvellous for sharing ideas, which was the purpose of Tim Berners-Lee, when he set up the world wide web so that scientists could communicate. Sadly, it is now widely abused by bullies out to publicly humiliate victims. At the time of writing, Katie Price is speaking to Parliament as part of her campaign to have cyber bullying made a criminal offence. Her autistic son has been subjected to gross abuse and this feisty lady is not taking this lying down. Hopefully Katie will succeed. At present, cyber bullies could be taken to a civil court, under the law of defamation. Unfairly this law is only accessible to those with the means to employ barristers.

Cyber bullies only denigrate themselves. A right-minded person would not indulge in gross behaviour which is offensive and psychologically damaging to the receiver. Many teenagers commit suicide because of cyber bullying which shames the community.

Likely Victims

A victim is selected for innumerable reasons; good looks, talent, nice personality, a popular individual with a wide circle of friends or an easy target like a disabled person. It might be the colour of your hair (Chris Evans was bullied for his red hair) to clothes, a skill or talent. Maybe you have a boyfriend/girlfriend while the bully does not. It could be you are popular and the bully wants to drive you out of that group. Or it might be, as in the film 'Carrie', the group are bent on finding a victim from malice. Sensitive, creative, studious or sporty – most likely you are over-forgiving and rarely 'rock the boat'. It is not you they are targeting but what you stand for in their eyes.

Common Signs of Cyber Bullying

Watch out if your child shows unusual behaviour:

1. sudden withdrawal from computer activity
2. bunking-off school
3. making excuses or telling lies
4. sudden change in communication e.g. reluctance to talk
5. sudden changes in mood, e.g. quiet, angry, hostile, withdrawn
6. self harm – or expressing suicidal ideas
7. Reduced quality of school work
8. lack interest in things which were a source of happiness
9. stop going out with friends
10. any rapid and unexplained change of friendships

There are plenty of anti bullying support groups online. Select one from the anti bullying charities (Refer resources) avoiding highly personalised sites. For serious cyber bullying report this to the police and your internet service provider. All decent service providers have a complaints section. If yours does not, consider changing provider.

FORMS OF CYBER BULLYING

Cyber-bullying is using the Internet to send text and/or images or symbols or symbolic languages, which threaten, frighten, torment or humiliate the target. This can be by email, in chat rooms, social networks (Twitter, WhatsApp, Facebook, Utube, Instagram, Snapchat), bulletin boards or websites with facilities for messaging or chatting.

Slang names for cyber bullying change frequently so keep up-to-date by checking anti-bullying websites. Beware commercial firms who pose as charities to sell services. Genuine registered charities offer free information and advice. Below are some of the current terms.

Stalking/harassing/'cyber stalking'

Cyber-stalking is similar to physical stalking, a miscreant following a victim with malicious or criminal intent. In cyber stalking the bully constantly emails, messages or uses chat which contains threats of harm or damage, to coerce a victim into doing something. This can be followed up with threatening to tell relatives, friends or post sexual images if the victim refuses. Though these are empty threats (adults would take action if they knew!) a vulnerable child or teen is easily seduced into believing. It is imperative to inform the police (see action for parents and helpers) and the internet provider. They will give advice and offer victim support.

Impersonating/masquerading/'fraping'/'catfishing'/'fake profile/'trickery'

This is a very serious crime where a bully takes over the identity of their victim with malicious intent, for example gaining access to the victim's social circle; obtaining bank details; isolating the victim from a group of which they are a valued member. This bully often uses the victim's profile to send false information to the victim's email or messaging list. The message will appear to originate from the victim. Millions of pounds have been defrauded from victims in this way.

Sexual shaming/'Bait out'/'dissing'/'outing'

Here the cyber bully reveals sexual secrets about their victim, true or made up, posting images which may have been doctored or making malicious claims about their sex life in text, abusive messaging or chat. These secrets may or may not be true (see also frenemy). 'Bait out' is where this is carried out by a group on an individual.

Provocation/'Trolling'/'flaming'

A victim is provoked by sending messages the sender knows will annoy, anger or inflame the victim. If sent to victims covered by hate crime this is a criminal offence. The sender uses crude sexual language or insults targeted to the victim's racial origin, religious belief, sexual orientation or disability.

Cyber Frenemy

A frenemy befriends a victim purely to obtain personal information, which they intend to pass to others to humiliate the victim. This malicious gossip is often spread over the internet. The frenemy gets a bargain, enjoying the benefits of friendship whilst getting kudos from avid gossip receivers. This is a particularly hurtful type of bullying as the victim loses trust. Teens especially need support for emotional hurt.

Dangers

Cyber bullying is far more serious than it seems and sadly commonplace. There is risk of long term psychological damage, damage to trust and a strong potential for it to trigger depression and suicide. Many cyber bullying activities are crimes. To repeat, this MUST be reported to the police as well as the internet service providers of sender and recipient, also to the head of the involved School[s].

Why Don't Victims Change Emails or Internet sites?

A common question of bewildered parents and helpers is, why don't victims stop going to the offending site or change email address? It is not that simple. A victim might have a long list of followers and it would be as difficult for them as for you to change your address book with the associated disruption, frustration, anger and so on. Moving away too quickly also sets up a wrong message, leading to potential reprisals and increase in the behaviour, as bullies perceive the victim's fear. The bully, having once discovered a victim's internet service provider details can find them again.

Strong measures are taken by decent ISP's (internet service providers) as they are by the police. Policiticans are aware prevalent this kind of bully behaviour has become thanks to campaigns by celebrities like Katie Price. Anne Longfield, the children's commissioner for England, called for a Government Ombudsman to be set up to mediate between social network firms and children having cyber issues. She called for "compulsory digital citizenship classes" in schools, which could be added to anti bullying measures schools are already legally obliged to have in place.

ACTION FOR VICTIMS:
Share worries and fears

Cyber bullying is not a named crime but there are criminal laws which cover such communications. ALWAYS report cyber bullying to the police (telephone 101, the non emergency police number). Remember, it is the bully who has a problem, not you.

Remember, even celebrity Katie Price's son is not immune from online creeps. Make sure your form teacher, school counsellor, the Head or classroom supporter knows what is happening. And DO maintain friendships. Anyone who walks away as a result of hearing gossip is not a true friend.

Online Safety
If you are computer savvy, great, but please read the following list and see if there is anything you might not be doing to keep yourself safe online (let me know if I missed anything via the publisher!):

* NEVER arrange to meet someone you met online without taking an adult AND
* do not believe what cyber bullies write. It is deliberate provocation.
* don't give out personal details. A hacker might identify you
* use a handle or nickname where ever possible
* don't answer any offensive emails or messages
* don't upload sensitive or sexual images or give personal information to anyone you only know through the internet
* do not upload text or images about anyone's sex life; this is a crime
* show a parent or teacher offensive text or images sent you
* no one can 'get you in trouble', a frequent claim of cyber bullies. they will be 'in trouble' when they are caught
* take great care when using social networks

Find a buddy
Every school must have anti bullying measures by law. Check out what is available in your school. If something is missing, like training, ask to be given it. Find a buddy, someone you can talk with confidentially. This might be an anti bullying ambassador,

a friend or someone else who has been bullied. Your buddy could be in or outside school, but it is vital to have someone you can confide in.

Have others networks to share with friends
Deflate cyber bullies by having several different networks or sites where you meet friends. That way, if they do manage to ruin one group, you will have backups. Maintain friendships outside school and do not stop going to groups, social or clubs that you enjoy. If you do give up, the bully has won because they want to isolate you. Follow advice in the previous section too. Remember this golden rule – it is the bully who has the problem, not you.

ACTION FOR PARENTS/HELPERS:
Take It Seriously
First and foremost, cyber-bullying is more common than you might imagine. It is easy for those who do not understand the glamour of the internet to say, 'oh, can't they just stop using it?' or some other faux solution. The fact is, this generation were brought up with computers, as each succeeding generation will have new trends. Didn't you? If you stop your kid from using the internet, you will be isolating them and giving the bully a weapon.

To anyone brought up with computers, using a laptop, i-pad or mobile phone is as essential as wearing the right clothes or joining the right groups or going to the right club. It means acceptance. Most of us have gone through being 'it' – chosen last when everyone is asked to form teams or feeling left out after not being invited to a party. Far better to talk, put safety measures in place and trust them enough to tell about what goes on. Do not criticise, just listen. Let the child know they are teaching you about something new and that will boost their confidence, far better than criticism or getting angry about the bullies.

If Your Child is a Cyber Bully

You cannot let this ride. Would you risk another mother's child committing suicide, because of something you failed to do? Sort it out rapidly. It is not easy to admit your child is a cyber bully whether an isolated incident or habitual. If they show no remorse, consider involving community police, who would rather deal with things informally than be investigating yet another bullycide.

Carolyn Bunting, general manager of Internet Matters, suggests parents talk to the child calmly without blame. Explain how being popular through uploading text and images that appear funny to others but hurt the target is morally wrong and could get them in trouble with the police. That cyber bullying is a crime and if anyone gets a reputation for this, their friends will not want to be involved with them in case they get in trouble too. Bunting advises not to take away the device but put a sanction on its use for mischief (e.g. grounding). It is counterproductive getting angry or blaming as this sends bullies underground. instead talk to them adult-to-adult, using their behaviour as a learning point rather than focusing on blame and punishment.

Online Safety

See also advice to victims, above. I am writing this for parents or helpers not savvy with computers, so bear with me if this does not apply. Most computer sites insist on safety such as passwords. These need to be kept secret and changed regularly. Make sure your child is doing this or let them show you on the pretext of showing you how to do it. Email systems like Google's gmail have a 'spam' box which filters out emails from addresses which do not appear in the child's email contact list – this is the electronic equivalent of an address book. Gmail is regularly updated by the provider and very good at ferreting out unknown emails. Make sure your child does not open spam emails, which will have been sent to numerous email addresses, not just your child. You can tell spam from the subject line which might be worded like one of these:

- 'You ignoring me [name from child's email address]?'
- 'Why you send me images like that?'
- 'This is a security note from your bank'
- 'Hey [child's name from email address]!'
- 'Open immediately' or 'very urgent'.
- 'stop sending me those images!'
- 'Security alert: someone has your password'
- 'If you wish to discontinue these emails, please respond'
- 'Are you [child's email address]?'

The sender tries to 'engage' by implying the receiver has done something wrong or making an insulting remark. They might masquerade as a commercial seller or implying there is a gift waiting. They might label the email urgent or address it 'as if' from a friend. If your child receives any such email, especially if it has an attached file, they must delete it. Attachments to spam emails can contain malicious code to stop computer programmes working properly. You can tell a file is attached by a paper-clip symbol alongside the email. Similarly, if emails arrive with no subject heading, don't open them. Your child could ask friends to use a coded subject title so they can identify each other. A number of measures make it difficult for miscreants.

There are parental controls on computers. If you do not

know how to use them, ask another parent. Among other things, parental control can block dangerous sites your child visits, ban offensive or adult-only pages and other useful safety settings. You can also contact anti bullying charities who have access to information. Many libraries run free understanding computer courses for adults and you can ask experts who run these courses for information.

Behavioural Changes and Emotions

Cyber bullying hits a victim emotionally. They may not show it outwardly but humiliation cuts deep, especially sexual bullying which is sexual harassment. Online bullying hurts as much as face to face. The danger of hurt and held-in emotions is that it leads to risk of depression and suicide. Depression is a common mental illness which can be triggered by emotional upheaval. Cyber bullying is a causal factor in child suicide (bullycide). If your child shows signs of being cyber bullied and they are not talking about it, act fast. Check with the school about marked changes in the quality or level of school work, recent changes in attitude or character. If there is any sign of prolonged low mood, take them to your GP or school counsellor – whichever is faster.

Keep All Evidence

Though information posted on the Internet appears ephemeral, a computer expert can recover deleted data. It is useful to let your child know this. The police use expert analysts to trace offenders. Author Stella O'Malley suggests taking screen shots of offensive material. Print them and keep copies locked away until there is enough material to hand to police and ISP (internet service provider). Your child might be more knowledgeable than you about computers so ask their help in ferreting information such as the ISP of the offender, their nickname (identity, user name, avatar) and if there is a pattern to the offending material. If age appropriate, point out this is the sort of work detectives do, so they are being their own Sherlock Holmes.

Make Sure Your Child is Not Isolated

Cyber bullies want to separate the victim from friends and allies. This is the first thing a bully does, to reduce the number of people watching out for the victim. Conversely, it is vital to ensure your child has plenty of alternatives for socialising online and offline. The wider their networks, the harder it will be for them to be isolated.

Another good idea from O'Malley is your child getting together with other bullied children to share experiences and support each other. Perhaps a site might be set up by a parent or someone in your family or the school. Everyone needs someone to talk to about problems. If the school sanctions it, perhaps anti bully ambassadors could take part in such a scheme overseen by a responsible adult.

Contact Internet Service Providers

It is vital to inform ISP's of concerns. If offensive material has been uploaded, demand it is taken down immediately. If they argue, report them to the police. Find out what measures they provide to prevent cyber bullying. If none, ask why. Social network sites like WhatsApp, Twitter, Utube, Instagram, Snapchat might be large companies but public support is vital to them. If any respond negatively, get with other parents and start a campaign, garnering support from local newspapers, e-newspapers and anti bullying charities (see resources). You have more power than you imagine and if you exercise this your child will notice and develop their own power.

Delete Days

As another arm to this issue, O'Malley suggests 'delete days' when everyone is encouraged to take down offensive or upsetting material. Maybe this can be tied to festivals, holidays, human rights campaigns or memorials to kids like Stephen Lawrence and other victims of bullying. This would be empowering for bully and bullied, encouraging forgiveness.

Though it might seem an uphill struggle and though cyber bullying is a factor of online life, do not let this prevent you and your child's enjoying being online. There is amazing stuff out there; free online courses from reputable universities, free news from BBC and a huge amount of research material from experts. You can even enjoy a virtual tour of Pompeii. People are incredibly generous sharing their expert information. The trick is to regularly visit only reputable sites, cooperate with the online community to weed out miscreants, use social networks with scepticism and practice STAYING SAFE at all times.

COMMENT

Katie Price's campaign to make cyber bullying a crime gathers momentum as 200,000 people sign her online campaign. Anyone can start a petition on Change.org or at 38Degrees (see Resources). After 100,000 signatures the Government will accept the signed petition and a question asked by your MP in Parliament. This is one of the first public forums which directly lead to changes in legislation. Justice and the law as many now believe are different entities. To get into court you need money, unless you come within that narrow band offered funding for Tribunals. Online anti-bullying initiatives always need support, as well as donations if that is possible for you. There is a huge amount of good on the internet despite its recent tarnished image. There will always be malice, not only on the internet. All we can do is keep fighting it.

* * *

SPACE FOR YOUR NOTES:

9: WORKPLACE BULLYING

- who bullies whom
- likely targets
- prevalence of bully behaviour
- FORMS OF WORKPLACE BULLYING:
- overt
- collusive
- HOW BULLIES GET AWAY WITH THEIR BEHAVIOUR
- toxic work environments
- the problem with Employment Tribunals
- FAIR DEALING
- taking an Employer to Tribunal
- WHAT TO DO – tips for EMPLOYEES
- what not to expect
- WHAT TO DO – tips for PROFESSIONALS
- Harvard Business Review – Dealing with toxic firms
- COMMENT

Who Bullies Whom

72% of workplace bullying is Managers on subordinates; perhaps not so high as you might expect. Less common is where manipulative or cry bully employees bully a manager, for example to get a disliked manager humiliated or ejected from post. There is bullying between management levels too as they jockey for position. Middle Managers fear rocking the boat in environments where they are vulnerable to being made redundant. It is easy for higher management to eject those they do not like, through legitimate restructuring programmes or manufactured situations. Permanent staff bully temporary staff, the latter particularly vulnerable because of their short term contracts and lack of legal redress. Temps do not earn enough to employ legal professionals unless this is provided as part of Union membership. That is why it is vital for temps to join a Union. Long term staff are likely to abuse newbies. Both temps and newbies will not have had time to learn how workplace systems and cliques operate and are vulnerable to all manner of bully behaviour, from covert threats to direct sexual harassment. There is very little they can do other than leave and hope the agency is willing (and able) to find alternative work. Larger institutions, the NHS, charities, forces and the police are prone to clique bullies. These individuals will have been in post a long time and know HR staff and systems inside out, knowledge which can easily be abused to remove victims from post. Whistleblowers (who reveal wrongdoing) are common targets as they threaten the lacunas bullies use.

Sociopaths in the workplace bully at all levels. These manipulative yet often intelligent, individuals lie, cheat, abuse and mask themselves all the way up the career ladder. Once outed, such individuals are rarely got rid of but are likely to be promoted to an obscure location where they cause HR less overt problems.

Likely targets

Employees who are different by dint of character, race, colour, belief, political orientation, disability, physically or through style, are likely targets. New and easy-going Managers are bullied in robust environments where long-term staff have hidden agendas. Particularly vulnerable are staff who have not or cannot easily learn hidden social rules, do not know the culture or have been in post less than two years and are therefore easy to dismiss. Conversely, staff with 'sexy' disabilities or disfigurements (i.e. prominent in current society) can be cosseted whilst staff not classed as 'cool' become substitute targets. I believe our modern social landscape with greater awareness of diversity is driving abuse onto less visible targets. Even bullies do not want to be badly perceived in the locality.

Prevalence of Workplace Bullying

Though workplace bullying is prevalent it is not yet widely researched. In 2015, TUC records show an estimated 1:3 of workers bullied, 72% by a manager, with 36% leaving post because of bullying (constructive dismissal). Of bullied-out employees, 34% are women and 23% men. In 2015, ACAS stated they were receiving up to 20,000 calls a year about workplace bullying. Bullying has been a taboo subject for many years but is being recognised because of greater media attention, for example about domestic violence and bullycides among children. Whistleblower law helps new employees gain relief it does not cover staff-on-staff bullying, where whistle blowing is not the prime causal factor. Lack of funding means whistleblower cases more than 2 years old have little chance of redress. Apart from whistleblower law and the new criminal offence of Hate Crime (refer, Bullying in the Community) there is no law for bullying per se. This makes it impossible for researchers to recover statistical records through courts. Union officials know there is huge suffering among ex-employees, many losing their livelihoods and homes. That many websites offer support for workplace bullying (see Resources) demonstrates this to be a wide-ranging problem.

FORMS OF WORKPLACE BULLYING

The bully behaviours below are representative yet not exhaustive. Bullies are good at innovating ways of tormenting. Such situations are well known to HR's, ACAS, Trades Unions and Tribunals. As it is, even HR's aware of bullying can fail to act. I will explain why later. Bully behaviours can be divided into two types; overt and collusive. Overt is behaviour carried out by the bully. Covert is where a bully colludes to attack the target. Often bully supports are not aware of what they are doing but have been manipulated. Covert Bully Behaviour is carried out where a bully believes witnesses cannot be bought or do not fear reprisals. Only a sociopath would bully in front of witnesses (overt bullying). The bully might invite a victim to stay after work on some pretext; perhaps implying a promotion or reward. With a victim closeted without witnesses, a bully can say or do what they like and deny it. That is why it is a good idea to carry a covert recording device if your manager is a bully. I did this in a meeting with such a one and HR; his outraged reaction was classic. These are examples of workplace bullying:

- shouting, hitting, crowding
- sexual harassment
- implying job at risk if victim does not comply
- cyber bullying
- being hyper critical of the victim and/or their work
- cry bullying – making a pretence of being bullied
- temporary staff threatened with termination of contract for not complying
- hiding, destroying or downplaying a victim's work
- leaving offensive notes for victim
- writing offensive slogans on victim's property
- sending or circulating offensive letters/emails about the victim

Shouting, hitting or crowding (moving very close to the target) are classic bully behaviours. These displays are less common with the advent of mobile cameras and recording devices offering sound evidence-gathering.

Psychological intimidation As with sexual harassment, a victim will be threatened with job loss, a poor appraisal or other easily trumped-up action if they do not concede to the demands.

Sexual harassment, of women and men, is any crude suggestions, touching, offensive sexual 'jokes', sexting, snide remarks about sexuality/lack of sex appeal. Improvement in social awareness and legislation has reduced taboos and increased reportage of this form of bullying. A group of female Hollywood stars recently organised the 'Me Too' campaign, following film Director Harvey Weinstein reputedly abusing the casting couch for many years.

Cyber bullying is making offensive remarks or posting offensive images of a victim via the internet, using a phone, computer or other connected device. Intranets are rife with this behaviour. This must be reported to the police. They will decide what reaction is best.

In **cry bullying**, a bully poses as victim to gain sympathy, to humiliate and punish the victim. Innocent bystanders or rescuers (refer diagram, Victim/Bully/Rescuer] are thus covertly recruited, a ploy that reveals a bully's devious nature. A bully never takes responsibility. That is the difference between a bully and someone who does not realize they are bullying (refer, Case Studies, HR Manager). Cry bullying is often used by bullies about to be outed.

Being **hyper-critical** is common during bully investigations. This process sensitises staff to certain traits of the victim which they tend to focus upon, to the exclusion of 95% of their reasonable behaviour. Chinese Whispers during these stressful periods make it difficult to track back the originator. This is why all documents and correspondence must be kept, if you are likely to need evidence for a Tribunal.

Collusive Behaviour is when a bully incites others to join in. This maximises hurt for the victim, at the same time increasing a bully's sadistic pleasure:

- spreading lies to humiliate / damage the target's reputation
- using known office gossips to spread malicious rumours
- demeaning victims through use of existing staff prejudice, e.g. abusing gay men to staff they know dislike homosexuals
- excluding the target in meetings, socials or online,
- not acknowledging a victim's contribution or work
- lying to HR about target's work / character / behaviour

Webs of collusion, deceit or Chinese whispers, malicious or not, are difficult for anyone to fathom, let alone naive HR personnel untrained in anti bullying measures. They are not experienced interviewers like ACAS staff or the police and tend to look only on the surface; at what they expect rather than what is. **Office gossips** spread rumours which add to the deceit. Why? Perhaps boredom or being disgruntled with the target and what the victim represents, or as a substitute revenge for imagined or historical hurts. Office gossips might be bullies-in-the-bud, waiting an opportunity to wield power. Toxic offices become rife with such individuals as morale lowers and decent staff leave. **Rumour Mongering** is difficult for HR's to fathom because cliques stick together. Staff with deep rooted prejudice are easy to manipulate, even otherwise intelligent people.

When a person of standing repeats gossip, seniors tend to believe them. This is known as 'the halo effect' and is why serious bully managers court HR and Union officials; to get their support system in place. **Bully Supports** or **Career Advancers** extend rumours. Once these reach higher management, everyone assume the person below them is passing truth. The halo effect is another reason disciplinary procedures ought to be dealt with by outside mediators.

HOW BULLIES GET AWAY WITH THEIR BEHAVIOUR

Bullies, often charming on the surface, find it easy to convince a gullible HR that the victim possesses characteristics which belong to the bully. An incompetent manager pins blame on their selected target thus focusing attention away from their own errors. This practice is so commonplace psychologists have a term for it – projection and splitting. The bully projects bad traits onto the victim, splitting off and owning only the good. Other terms describing this practice are the halo or goddess effect. Once an employee has been dubbed with a bad reputation, regardless of the truth, the first impression sticks. Newbies and outsiders are particularly vulnerable.

Hardened bullies are clever and manipulative. To shift them costs a great deal, is difficult and will be bad for a firm's reputation. That is why HR's often promote the bully before sending them to a distant office where they can do the least harm. Toxic firms spend thousands on employment legal experts to keep employee complaints out of court. I heard this often from the TUC, legal experts, tribunal staff and other bullied employees. An employee seems more expendable than a manager but by ridding themselves of decent staff whilst retaining bullies, a firm risks implosion and ruin.

Manipulating HR Systems

These methods are used to oust whistle-blowers:

- threats of redundancy, job loss, demotion, worse work conditions
- biased reporting on appraisals and other HR reports
- untruthful performance managements (based on above)
- labelling victim; 'difficult', 'obstructive', 'manipulative' or 'refusing to take part in disciplinary procedures'
- halo effect i.e. 'poor-me' manager / 'difficult' staff

- collusion among a clique of seniors
- disciplinary procedures carried out in absence of victim
- ensuing procedures make smoke cloud, masking original bullying

Toxic Workplaces

A toxic workplace can be identified by:

- frequent in-fighting
- lack of leadership
- no values/controls
- staff have no or little say in the running of the organisation
- implied threats (e.g. job loss or redundancy if anyone dares to 'speak out')
- malicious gossip

In toxic environments staff are always de-motivated, stressed/ depressed and likely to form protective cliques. This leads to sickness absence, duvet days and physical symptoms of stress (high blood pressure, headaches, fainting, diabetes, heart attack, stroke). The result? More absence, less engagement, more accidents, lower profit, frequent complaints/litigation and in-fighting. This triggers high staff turnover and a bad reputation. Highly motivated individuals will not be attracted. But many toxic firms did not begin that way. Any firm can turn toxic:

- too much pressure leading to stressors
- lack of profit / funding / income
- no money to recruit new staff
- unhealthy competition between factions
- raised hours and increased workload
- authoritarian managers & no employee power sharing
- managers encouraging in fighting
- whistle-blowers castigated rather than listened to
- malicious gossip among cliques

- newcomers derided/treated with suspicion/ new ideas unwelcome
- no follow up to complaints by burnt-out HR
- disinterest or collusion among senior managers
- whistle blowing discouraged with draconian measures
- e.g.: threat of job loss, redundancy or worse conditions

In hotbeds, wrongdoers blame scapegoats, whereas in decent environments, staff resolve problems through talking.

The Problem with Employment Tribunals

Senior HR staff are surprisingly ill informed of the complex processes in bullying. This is clear from packed Tribunals and litigants-in-person, as well as Trade Union officials, Government-appointed Whistleblower Guardians and legal advice bureaus. Under current law ACAS mediation can be refused without penalty. Tribunals are aware of semi-legal loopholes which breach Article 8 of the Human Rights Act:

- deliberate delays over disclosure of documents
- missing/altered documents
- sending a litigant so much paperwork they cannot cope
- hearings held in a litigant's absence –
- legal team manipulating a Judgement in the litigant's absence
- deliberate delaying until a case runs out of time
- obfuscating; frightening victims with legal language
- threatening huge legal costs if employee attempts to take a Tribunal
- hectoring by barristers
- using wig, gown & 'aura' to intimidate litigant in court

I was informed by Tribunal staff that some 40% of applicants have no legal representation whereas employers always do. Civil courts do not provide free or low cost legal aid which leaves litigants in an impossible battle for justice. Court systems are antiquated, complex and notoriously slow:

- too many forms in overblown language
- explanatory leaflets as extensive as tomes, often needing cross referral
- archaic procedures
- expensive & fee exemptions for few situations
- long delays due to lack of court staff
- ACAS mediation rarely complied with by toxic firms
- Judges do not use plain English or allow applicant to question BEFORE judgement
- Barristers hector or decimate litigant's character
- expert staff fear a barrister making them look foolish or unprofessional

The antiquated UK legal system has long been criticised. Justice and the law are not the same thing. William Shakespeare's complaint of, 'the law's delay.. the insolence of office' is extant. Read a typical expose of court delays in Charles Dickens magnificent novel, 'Bleak House,' and he might be speaking of today's legal system. Legal people might claim their system 'tried and tested over hundreds of years.' Sadly, it is proven only to keep legal staff employed and pay expensive fees. Civil law has long been a means for rich people annoy each other, not for everyday folk to find justice and closure. Barristers get paid if they win or lose. As a Judge once said to me, barristers rarely take on cases that are not likely to succeed. The few who take pro bono (charity or free work) often do so because the case is interesting i.e. brings up an interesting or topical point of law. The 'free half hour' is no longer in vogue but always was a means of legal firms finding new clients.

Any Psychologist knows stress will hit a victim (scapegoat). This has been known since the rise of psychology. Boards are remote and expect senior HR to resolve employment problems on their behalf, without being directly involved. This lays HR open to abuse. Documents and reports can easily be altered or disappeared; the wrong staff chosen for investigations; conclusions written by biased seniors. So what, if anything can be done to prevent this? I outline suggestions on my website but here is a summary:

FAIR DEALING – A Suggested Preventative System

1. **Compulsory Dispute Mediation by ACAS.** HR would need to explain to ACAS reasons for non compliance and being penalized for this. This prevents powerful institutions like the NHS refusing mediation.
2. **Performance management overseen by external mediators.** Documentation rubber-stamped only with claimant's consent.
3. **Dignity at Work** investigations conducted by **ACAS**, waiting for individuals to recover before interview (major decisions should not be made during after-shock).
4. **grievance conducted by ACAS**. Prevents evidence tampering. Enables expert advice in the case of disability.
5. **legal funding removed**– redistributed to ACAS to pay for increased staffing and legal advice.
6. **legal advice by ACAS-employed professionals** to estimate damages.
7. **ACAS report to Tribunal** with input from Trades Union representative where claimant so wishes.
8. **Judicial settlement** (binding on all parties). Prevents lengthy, expensive and traumatic Tribunals and reduces time factor. Prevents evidence-tampering.

This system improves on current systems:

- more cost effective than current system
- nip disputes in the bud, reducing stress
- prevent lengthy waiting between dispute and Court
- less traumatic for staff and more confidential
- Prevent HR being involved in major disputes & prevent bias
- Prevent missing or tampered evidence / hearsay

In this system, no professionals would lose status:

- ACAS would increase staff thus reduce waiting time
- Unions would still provide representation
- legal staff redeployed from in-house arrangement

If you feel this system would work, please visit my website and copy my proposal to your MP.

Taking an Employer to a Tribunal

Whole books have been written on this subject so I'll offer a summary. Courts are used to individuals taking their own case and make allowances for presentation and lack of legal or procedural knowledge. There are guidance notes, some good some so extensive you need weeks to read them. There is a certain amount of funding if you are of limited means, this being linked to income. Go online or call Tribunal staff and ask for the correct form. Getting the right form is essential for Tribunals.

It is essential to look at time limits as these are strictly adhered to. If you are late completing a form you have to complete other forms to explain why, another fee exemption, then a Judge decides if this is allowable. Also, everything has to be backed with evidence. Think police procedural. If your boss hit you, you need a witness statement, a statement from yourself and photographs of injuries with hospital notes. This is how courts operate and there is no getting round it.

If you have been wise and joined a Union, they offer free

legal advice. If you are not in a Union, they might allow you to join if you pay the back fees. It is worthwhile as legal fees are expensive and pro bono rare. Private solicitors no longer offer a free half hour and many Citizens Advice Bureaus no longer offer legal help. Without legal representation the going will be very hard. If someone is willing to help with paperwork, let them but do not rely on them.

Check dates, forms and that these have been received. Online, courts send an auto receipt; keep these until the case is over. Send all else by recorded delivery, keeping copies of everything. Be prepared for a long process. This can take months, often a year. I found it useful to make a plan and tick off the steps so I could see progress. Like any journey, you get tired and need to sit down and review. Over time you gain confidence, learn to deal with court officials and speak to astute Judges.

For your day in Court take a friend as well as a Union / legal representative. Even with understanding Judges procedures will be stressful. Dress soberly but do not overdress. Judges are looking not only at evidence but signs of your personality and behaviour toward others.

Thank yourself for proceeding with Tribunal. You are not only helping yourself but adding to the store of knowledge kept by courts and Government. Without such knowledge, research is impossible. It is only research that makes systems fair and workable. If you are given settlement the amount will not reflect all you have suffered, so do not expect it. If you win, be thankful. If not, remember winning is not the only goal. It is an achievement to be a part of the wider picture; accountability and fairness and laws to back that up. If you 'lost' there is the chance of appeal, counter appeal and so on. But do you want to find yourself in litigation for years? Becoming a campaigner is not easy. You risk being insulted, ignored, browbeaten, blacklisted and condemned as an 'ambulance chaser' as well as ignored by colleagues fearful of losing their job. Your friends might get worn out and desert you. You might never work in the field again. The rewards on the other side are tremendous. When you speak out against workplace injustice it is confidence boosting.

WHAT TO DO – TIPS FOR EMPLOYEES
Do Not Do Nothing
First it is VITAL to report bullying; to HR, a line Manager and a Union official.

Reporting bullying in itself is empowering. Stewing is not good for physical or mental health and is a trait of victimhood. Therefore:

- contact an Employee Assistance Programme at your firm if there is one
- if your Manager is the bully, go up-line until someone listens
- speak to a Union representative
- tell family and close friends
- seek other bullied staff who might be willing to report it
- do not gossip about the bully but go about your work quietly
- do not give up on hobbies, interesting or project, during the reporting process

Go further up the line until you receive a response. If your Union official is allied with a bully Manager, ask for a different representative. When you make waves, senior staff will focus on you. Be careful how you communicate or you might find yourself labelled a trouble maker.

Victims are NOT weak
Never listen to the old adage, 'victims are 'weak'. A bully selects targets with something about them; something they envy. Their

aim is to get rid, so they do not have to face someone they perceive 'better' than them. Bullying becomes their expert subject. A bully gets kicks from behaviour which reduces their victim. If you do not react emotionally, they will usually find an easier target (unless they are a sociopath).

Record All Instances of Bullying
Record all bullying. Keep the log away from prying eyes. I would keep it awhile before showing HR; you need to find out which staff can be trusted. In a toxic firm, otherwise decent staff will kow-tow to the bully, who will have a wide circle of supporters (bully supports). This is why you must get professional support. These are level one actions – do them straight away.

If the Firm is Toxic, Consider Leaving
If the firm is toxic there is little you can do. Going it alone under these circumstances is futile and will ruin your confidence and mental health. Watch for high staff turnover, a classic sign of a toxic firm. If your career is niche, get out before you lose a good reference. Blacklisting of ousted professional employees is commonplace. Toxic HR's want to avoid flames from shareholders / Boards and secure their position. Look for the positive; work for yourself or choose a new aspect in your field of work. Life after bullying can be positive if you take new opportunities.

Keep Networks Alive
Do not neglect social networks even if you don't feel up to going out. If you try to go out most of the time you will be pleased you made the effort. Likewise, keep friends and family in the loop. If friends do not want to hear your worries or are constantly busy, let them go. Some find it hard to cope with

emotions, even their own, so do not blame yourself. It is always possible to start afresh.

Find Professional Support

It is vital to find support like counselling or appointments with a GP to look for signs of stress-related illnesses. We often forget body and mind are linked; what affects one affects the other. There is little funding for individual counselling but you might be offered 6 to 8 sessions, extended if you are lucky. Otherwise, GP surgeries offer stress management courses. These are useful and give you an insight into human behaviour. They are free and held in the evenings. Levels 3 and 4 in this book contain the basics; understanding stress and its links with fight-fight-flight syndrome; the triangle of insight; mindfulness and self help (level 1).

There might be a Wellbeing College in your locality. These centres offer free courses to help you relax and get out in the fresh air, proven to be beneficial to health. These are funded by local authority and health commissioners.

Do not be put off if your GP suggests a psychiatric appointment. Bullying is known to adversely affect mental health and it is vital that any sign of depression is treated. A Psychiatrist is an expert in medication for anxiety, depressive illness and other mental conditions exacerbated by stress. Many Psychiatrists are also trained in counselling. Whereas a GP has 10 minute appointments, a psychiatric appointment lasts 50 minutes to an hour. This extended time is vital for patients to explain what is happening and enable diagnosis. An assessment is taken by a member of a local mental health team. An appropriate mental health worker will be appointed and can visit at home if you prefer. In many cases they offer support until the problem is resolved. There is no stigma and this is useful evidence if you begin a Tribunal.

Analyse Why the Bully Envies You

Listen to what the bully is criticising. It will often be a negative of a skill, talent or personality trait. If for example they say you have bad presentation, look in the mirror with a friend. Are you really as they say or is it jealousy? Jealousy expresses itself with negative eyes; it is your task to find the positive. Another example – are they saying you are not doing your fair share of work? Is that true or are they doing as little as possible. In either case, positively critique yourself. If they say you are rude to customers, perhaps you have a talent for customer service. The bully wants to prevent you doing things you are good at. Conversely, if you are being scapegoated (victimised) for existing problems, get peer support and where possible go as a group to HR to complain. If you have been selected as victim, do not be down hearted because there is always something positive to learn from a bully's actions, to help you improve your future life.

What Not to Expect / What Not to Do

Be prepared for the negative. Do not be shocked if colleagues do not support you. They might fear consequences, for example not being believed or in case the bully retaliates. Many individuals live at basic level and when things go wrong they can't cope. These are Pollyanna's (see films in Resources) who see everything in a rosy glow. They are not realistic and not helpful. Second, **things will not always be like this**. Bully situations are uncomfortable but pass. If no one helps **find a better job**, but find one before leaving – do not walk out on a whim. Losing your home because you can't pay the mortgage is no picnic and you do not want financial worries on top of everything else. **Get a good reference**, get a better job, start working then see if you want to deal with the bully. Even years later you can do this, as a way of letting go.

WHAT TO DO – TIPS FOR PROFESSIONALS

A bully manager will be determined to oust their victim. This is something which all HR's ought be aware. Bullying based on fake appraisals is less easy if you insist managers put everything in writing, as with the victim. It is your job to deal with the bullying, do not renege. Do not get personal and do not favour one party, even if you know them well. Imagine this is happening to a friend or relative; how would you want it deal with? Listen before acting. If you are likely to be biased, go up the chain and ask for someone else to deal with it. Judges of the highest calibre step aside if they know they have a bias. There is no shame in this.

It is vital for HR's to offer pastoral support to the protagonist, victim and all involved staff. Do not blame; look for cause not effect. For example, ask what triggered the bullying; can it be righted? If it is a wider issue, inform those who might be able to do something up the chain. Remember, even HR are not expert interviewers, like the police or ACAS. Do not let things slide. Your decisions can have lasting effect on others and ruin lives if you get it horribly wrong. Being an HR Officer is difficult and an HR Manager role should not be given a new recruit, no matter how experienced. Subtleties take time to seep in – and bullying is a very complex issue.

Anti Bullying Training

Anti bullying education is vital for staff, HR and senior managers. During interviews for the case studies in this book, it emerged one trainee psychologist was informed, 'we expect people to deal with this kind of thing.' An HR manager I interviewed said managers are shocked when informed they have been bullying staff. 'It takes the wind out of their sails,' he commented. Though denial is expected, he believes some managers are unaware of their behaviour; an old 'bull and army' attitude. He thought it a good idea for bullying to be covered during inductions.

Staffing Agencies
Many temporary workers find themselves targeted for bullying. They are vulnerable with few contacts to support them and often no Union. Agencies are in business to make profit and unlikely to side with workers against clients, even on health and safety issues. Contracts can be withdrawn as the business is highly competitive. You will not find much employment law practised in temporary agencies as there are always more temps than jobs. There is no redundancy and no come back. Temporary staff should register and keep in contact with as many agencies as possible. False loyalty does not pay a mortgage.

It would be better for the Government to implement legislation for licensing of agencies and improving employment law for all situations including false self employment contracts, zero hours contracts and paying a pittance rate to trick temporary staff to give up holiday rights. Unions are looked on with suspicion by agencies and firms paying national minimum wage and membership discouraged. Union membership is vital for temporary workers. Government employed mystery shoppers would prove useful to counteract these evils.

Harvard Business Review – Dealing with Toxic Employers
This is a summary of a podcast interview with Nicholas Pearce, Associate Professor of the School of Management, North-western University, USA:

1. people do not 'have the language' to describe toxic workplaces:
2. they refer to 'nasty gossip', stress or dislike going to work

3. changing a culture takes great commitment
4. a decent firm allows free expression of emotion
5. toxic organisations need to conduct analyses, engaging all staff
6. the problem is in the firm's mindset, not in individuals
7. the attitude of the CE is particularly important
8. whistle-blowers do risk job loss
9. altering small detail can help change the culture
10. individuals being recognised improves morale
11. employees need to have meaning in their work
12. encourage managers who have been bullied to help change things
13. likewise, present them as problem solvers, not problem makers
14. find committed others to form a group of change agents
15. failure to carry out 14. risks ideas being blocked
16. the individual who sparks change also risks job loss
17. the firm needs leaders committed to change
18. have exit interviews for all leavers

COMMENT

There are many facets to workplace bullying which makes it complex and time-consuming. This is why HR's and Boards seek over-simple solutions instead of discovering the truth over time. The best resolutions are focused on the positive, the worst seek blame. The current system with biased reportage, blame-seeking, the high cost of legal professionals and staff stress, needs overhaul. The Americans are way ahead on ideas judging by the Harvard podcast above. There needs to be research on all aspects of bullying, including days lost to industry, potential solutions as well as mental distress and suicides as outcomes of workplace bullying. Bullying is not yet listed on fit notes, making statistics difficult to discover. Small changes in HR systems with check backs could be implemented. Ex-employees can feedback via exit interviews and by reporting bullying post employment. HR's need to listen; set up anti bullying training for themselves and staff; deal promptly with issues; not use easy scapegoats to 'sort out' hot spots. MP's in dealing with constituent work complaints need to hire more staff or find volunteers rather than caving in to firms who fail to cooperate. The new Police Act makes it easier to tackle bullying in the community (anti social behaviour). It would be good to see similar support systems to counteract workplace bullying. Meanwhile, it is vital to report bullying, to not give up and tread carefully to protect loved ones from consequences.

* * *

SPACE FOR YOUR NOTES:

10: BULLYING IN FAMILIES

- who bullies whom
- likely victims
- Forms of domestic abuse
- Munchausen's and Munchausen by Proxy
- why family abuse goes unreported
- why family abuse must be reported
- signs of emotional abuse
- What to do
- Recognising abuse through emotional reactions
- COMMENT

Who Bullies Whom

Domestic violence is a form of bullying. Often fuelled by alcohol or drugs, it can also be triggered by extreme stress. There are a growing number of reports about female abusers. With decreasing taboo and more reporting of husbands attacked, more males are coming forward. Throughout history, domestic violence has been perceived as a male preserve. Up too Victorian times, chastisement of a wife and children was socially acceptable and considered a moral duty. Children were said to be born with original sin without the capacity to feel, like animals. This is why you read in Victorian autobiographies such as Kilvert's Diary attitudes which today would be considered abusive. Even well-loved writer Lewis Carroll is now viewed as dubious for taking photographs of naked children under the age of consent.

Likely victims

Stress might be taboo in middle and upper classes but violence and sexual abuse happens behind lace curtains. Consider the well-publicised case of Lady & Lord Lucan. it is well researched that an abused husband or wife often generates an abused child, who generates their own abused child and so on down the generations. Though it is difficult to have empathy for hardened criminals, it is reasonable to remember that many of these individuals were horrifically abused as children. There is a strong link between deprived homes, lack of social skills, little opportunity, low employment and bad press but abuse nevertheless happens in all kinds of domestic circumstances.

Children, step children, grandparents and distant relatives have all been victims of domestic abuse. Overcrowding, poverty, lack of paid work and financial problems can contribute to fatal outbursts. Elderly family members moving back to a daughter or son because of illness or poverty are vulnerable to verbal, physical and sexual abuse. It is hugely stressful caring for someone with disability or memory loss.

In the West care-giving is no longer seen as duty. This is in stark contrast to many African states wrongly dismissed as socially backward. Bereft of status, elderly individuals become as vulnerable as children and subjected to similar abuse, even sexual abuse, which is often an expression of power not lust.

FORMS OF DOMESTIC ABUSE
Victims are often so used to familial abuse they do not see it as wrong. That is why it is vital to learn its nuances. For simplicity, I have classified the behaviours into groups (though there are overlaps):

Physical abuse
- punching
- kicking
- stabbing
- slow poisoning

Sexual abuse
• rape
• forced incest

Psychological abuse
• threats
• deliberate humiliation
• isolating victim from family and friends
• power games by abusers with Munchausen's By Proxy

Emotional abuse
• being kind to others but never the victim
• claiming to love the victim whilst abusing them
• damaging relationship through lying / malicious gossip

Physical abuse

Read any report into the death of an individual at the hands of a family member and you will be horrified. Children, adults, even babies have been subjected to torture, often over considerable time, before being murdered by parents or adults known to the family. Sadistic behaviour is not the preserve of sociopaths and psychopaths. Such behaviour often hides a trail of abuse going back decades. A high proportion of serial prisoners have fat social services files. Small wonder child killers are placed in solitary confinement for protection from other prisoners. As Philip Larkin tellingly wrote, 'they fuck you up, your mum and dad.'

In some cases sadistic abuse is centred around outmoded historical belief; witchcraft, ancestor worship, voodoo, spirits (refer diagram, 'Child Deaths Through Family Abuse'). In July 2015, the Government set up an enquiry into child sexual abuse after the Jimmy Savile scandal. This has been re-convened twice with four new chairs and the pressure group, 'Survivors of

Organised and Institutional Abuse,' dropping out in despair. Up to March 2018, the Enquiry had read some 139,000 documents, heard 188 witnesses and received 1.5 million pages of evidence. In 2016 the Daily Mail demanded documents under FOI and discovered 288 children had been murdered in abuse cases SINCE The Children Act.

Sexual abuse

Familial sexual abuse is the rape of a child, adult or senior member of the family by a parent and includes all types of degrading sexual acts. There are two known reasons for this behaviour. The first is sexual; sexual predation to satisfy an urge of lust. This is likely to be individuals with high sex drives attracted to paedophilia (*sex with children under the age of consent*). Paedophiles indulge in sex with their own children as well as those outside the family. Think Fred and Rose West who sexually abused their children before murdering and burying them in their own garden.

The other reason for rape is power. Taking control of someone's body, particularly a child, gives the attacker a sense of domination and control, where they are unable to control other areas of their life. Outside families, degrading sexual behaviour is commonly requested of prostitutes by high standing members of society. Read the revealing book, 'Cynthia Payne: the Life and Work of An English Madam,' a copy of which Mrs Payne sent to the Judge who sentenced her in the hope he would expand his narrow view and 'learn something.' Sadism and masochism have been attributed to deviant sexual behaviour among public school tutors who took pleasure caning young male pupils, before corporal punishment was banned in schools. Research proves deviant behaviour in childhood leads to deviancy in adulthood.

Another kind of familial sexual abuse is where one or both parents force a child to have sexual relations with a sibling, which is termed, forced incest. Forced incest is a voyeuristic experience for the abuser, as is inducing children to take off their clothes and other covert sex acts. Incest has been a criminal offence in the UK for a long time. Under the Sexual Offences Act, 2003 incest is now termed, familial abuse. This wider definition includes abuse by foster parents or live-in partners. The law now views any sex act on a child of 13 or below as rape.

Psychological Abuse
Psychological abuse leaves victims emotionally scarred often ruining their chance of making loving relationships. This abuse of trust ranges from implied threats to deliberately humiliating victims, for example, forcing a child to wear dirty or inappropriate clothing not because of poverty but to shame the child. Deliberate humiliation in front of family or friends, denial of talents or achievements, being kind to outsiders whilst punishing the target in private, with or without sinister pre-warning are all psychological abuse or power games as Berne called them. Precious items might be taken or damaged or given away with smiling denial of wrong-doing. The victim might be denied access to friends through withholding messages, destroying letters and poisoning relationships. The aim is to make the victim believe no one cares for them except the abuser, a system also used by paedophiles in grooming children. Read Vladimir Nabokov's classic novel, 'Lolita' for a paedophile perspective.

Munchausen and Munchausen by Proxy
Munchausen and Munchausen by Proxy are recognised personality disorders. In the first, an individual feigns a physical

or mental illness to get attention and love. In the second form the abuser feigns or induces physical or mental illness in a child. Victims have been poisoned, had urine samples doctored with glucose and been wounded with dirt rubbed in to induce infection. In one famous case, a daughter was confined to a wheelchair then 'presented' by the mother as physically disabled for many years. The daughter went on to murder her mother. The abuser is usually a parent or a medical professional.

Why Family Abuse Goes Unreported

There are many reasons families are reluctant to reveal one or more of the family is being abused:

- disbelief/denial -'it's not happening', he /she loves me'
- hoping it will resolve by itself over time
- each incident is attributed as a mistake or one off incident i.e. 'it's only because x'
- shame/humiliation – 'what if neighbours/relatives/ employer get to know'; fear it might affect reputation, job, social standing, public life e.g. politician, celebrity
- misperceived as a class issue – 'only happens in deprived families'
- misperceived as 'normal' if abuse runs in the family
- false loyalty – 'keep it in the family'
- misperceived/false glow – 'he/she loves me in other ways'
- part of addictive behaviour – 'it will stop when they stop drinking/drug taking'

'We don't need help,' in a problem family masks denial. From time immemorial family problems have been seen as personal, not the concern of the state. But in a society with a welfare state there is moral obligation for the state to intervene. Sometimes the abuse has gone so many generations it is perceived as normal by the family. It is not only the wrong doer who sees it as normal but the victim. Children often don't realize they have been abused until they talk outside the family at primary school. This is where an abused child can become a bully or a target. Abuse is often misperceived as love by victims. Some victims would rather be abused than left isolated. Abusers feed into this by offering an occasional taste of 'love'; a gaudy trinket, a kiss or unexpected present. The victim will wait a long time, often years, for another treat. The abuser will withhold 'love' for longer and longer periods, cruelly extending hope until the last spark of rebellion dies or a despairing victim commits suicide. The elasticity of hope is a terrible weapon of a sociopath.

Why Family Abuse Must Be Reported
It is vital for all abuse to be reported. Vulnerable adults are classed as anyone with physical or mental impairment such that they are unable to fend for themselves. Examples of impairments are mental illness, sensory disorders, autism, learning disability, physical disability, incapacity due to blindness, deafness or ageing. Where the abused family have children, police and social services play key roles. Child abuse is a criminal offence as well as socially repugnant. Many abusive families are known to key agencies although, given extensive human rights it is difficult for them to act. Known abusers are recorded on a register then tracked. Technically this should deter potential offenders but child abuse is increasingly difficult to detect. The 'nosy neighbour' decried on one hand can save children from attack.

To secure conviction courts need cast iron evidence, for example bruised face, broken limb[s] or emotionally-scarred children wetting themselves in Court. They need evidence of abuse over time, particularly from social workers. That is why police monitor past and potential offenders. The balance of evidence and human rights can allow offenders to slip through the net. But it is empowering for victims to witness a miscreant brought to justice, no matter the time gap.

WHAT TO DO
Child Victims
If you are being abused you must get support. If you don't know how to do this, ask a trusted friend or their parent. As soon as you report abuse, you come under the protection of the law. Do not worry about being criticised or 'found out' by the abusive person. If you intend to go home, you will be given a social worker to support you. If it is unsafe to go home, any help agency will make sure you get to a place of safety. You can go to school and not lose contact with friends. Don't worry about clothes, food, money or a place to live as a professional will sort this out. They will not leave you to fend for yourself.

If you ring Childline you may have to ring a long time as there are not enough volunteers. This will change when they get more funding. If you get no reply, go to a teacher, school helper, school employee or head and tell them what is happening. You can ring or go to a local social services office. If you are being followed, go to a public place like a library, council offices, housing association and ask for help. You can also ring 101 and ask a community police officer to meet you. If it is night or urgent, ring 999 and ask for police help. Your abusive parent/relative/sibling will not be given your new location or telephone number. No one will criticise you and you will be safe.

Adult Victims
Adult victims, male, female, transgender and homosexual can contact Women's Aid for help. An internet search or local library will have area-specific resources. Local Authorities commission

different services so the names of organisations are not the same across the UK. There are refuge shelters nationwide where you just turn up. If you call the police they will take you to a shelter if you wish. Do not refuse if you have been hit, not even if your partner cries or promises never to hit you again. If possible take basic clothing, underwear and washing kit but do not worry as shelters have supplies. The shelters will take your children so do not worry about being separated. The days of 'Cathy Come Home' (see Resources, films) are long gone.

In a shelter you will find others who have been abused. You do not have to share information and your privacy will be protected. A member of staff will ask what you need, whether professional help, help with money, housing, information or social support. This may take a few days so be prepared to wait. You can stay at the shelter knowing you are safe. The addresses of refuges are confidential and there are plenty of people around if trouble occurs. Abusers are not allowed past the door.

Friends/Neighbours/Other Helpers

If you suspect abuse it is vital to report your fears to police or Social Services. CCTV, audio tapes, photographs and written testimony will help bring miscreant[s] to justice. If you are unsure whether you have witnessed abuse, report it anyway and let professionals decide. Do not confide your fears to others as this might result in vigilantes taking the law into their hands.

Make sure an abused person gets immediate help as above. Whilst help is coming, reassure them. Listening is the best thing you can do. If the abuser is nearby or the abused fears they are about to arrive, call 999 and the police will get the abused person and their children to a shelter. If they want you to go with them for reassurance, never reveal the address of a shelter.

The abuse might have been going on before the abused seeks

Diagram 2:
CHILD DEATHS THROUGH FAMILY ABUSE

1945	Denis O'Neill
1973	Maria Colwell
1973	Stephen Meurs
1975	Neil Howlett
1977	Wayne Brewer
1978	Darryn Clarke
1979	Paul Brown
1984	Heidi Kosedi
1984	Jasmine Beckford
1984	Tyra Henry
1986	Kimberley Carlile
2000	Kennedy McFarlane
2000	Victoria Climbie
2002	Ainlee Walker
2005	Deraye Lewis
2007	Baby P
2008	Hylene Essilfie
2013	Daniel Pelka
2014	Ayeeshia Jane Smith
2018	Jordan Burling

March 2016
'Child Death Enquiries will be overhauled' say Ministers'

"We now need clear action by national government to reform our framework for multi-agency arrangements and improve learning from serious events involving children.

We need a more effective statutory framework, reward initiative and innovation and ensure both of these are focused on supporting and developing our practitioners to improve the services provided to protect children and young people."

Daily Mail: '*288 child murders SINCE The Children Act*'

help. Do not ask them why the delay and do not be surprised if they express love for the abuser. Abused individuals will be confused about their emotions. For this reason do not criticise, judge or verbally attack the abuser even if the abuse described is horrific. If they are in shock, call an ambulance as well as police. Even on a warm day, shock sends blood from the skin's surface which causes shivering so make sure they have a blanket or extra covering. Tea is comforting but do not offer alcohol.

Ask when they last ate because shock can result in forgetfulness. A sandwich helps restore lost energy. The victim might be embarrassed particularly if there is no obvious mark or injury. If they are reticent or 'keep themselves to themselves' ask no questions. Keep to practicalities, do not recriminate, be calm, do not take sides – doing this is supportive though you may not think it enough. The professionals deal with all else. Finally, it is not your problem to tackle the abuse, though victims can try to involve outsiders. If you must 'do something,' raise funds for Women's Aid or Childline.

Recognising Abuse Through Emotional Reactions

For victims, this questionnaire offers a way to recognise abused

- ➤ do you always feel like an underdog or uncomfortable when the person is around?
- ➤ are your successes downplayed or the subject changed if you describe achievements?
- ➤ if you pour out your heart does the other seem nonchalant or give platitudes?
- ➤ do they encourage you to talk about abuse then enjoy your discomfort?
- ➤ do they ask personal, sexual or emotional detail, focusing on this rather than trying to understand events?

- do they make you go over and over detail, particularly sexual, claiming they 'need to understand'?
- Have possessions been broken or go missing when a certain person is around?
- have you queried this and been told you are over-sensitive or imagining it?
- do they prefer to hear things that went wrong, with or without false sympathy?
- are messages not passed on that jeopardise friendships or relationships?
- do any of the family relate spiteful gossip about you on the pretext of helping?
- are you told you are loved whilst your gut feeling says you are not?
- are you aware of manipulation through gut feelings?
- is this person always late, letting you down, breaking promises, finding excuses, preventing you attending longed-for events e.g. hiding tickets, 'forgetting' phone calls or messages or cancelling events at the last minute?
- does a lover hit you then apologise, promise not to do it again but begins again?
- is a partner always shower-fresh after returning late from work?
- do you feel blamed or impelled to apologise for things you have not done?
- are you corrected or belittled in front of friends or colleagues?
- are you told negative things in a jokey way, for example that your clothes are tight or being unfavourably compared with a friend?
- is teasing becoming more hurtful and regular?
- are you negatively compared with people then 'encouraged' to be like them?

These are all signs of emotional abuse. It is often easier to talk to a counsellor than to talk with a friend about abuse. There is less inhibition and the professional will not judge you. It is important to have support when you recognise emotional abuse, particularly of teenagers. Watch out if you are a friend or carer for signs of depression in a child or teenager when they realize they are being emotionally abused.

COMMENT

Reading reports and enquiries it soon becomes clear that many deaths might have been prevented if professionals had not been naive, agencies worked together and information shared. It is clear similar mistakes are made time and again. Effective changes have been made in the new Police Act (refer, Bullying in the Community), which ought to be applied to child protection and adult familial abuse:

- multi agency information sharing
- legal powers devolved to all involved agencies
- right of entry
- power to act in specific circumstances without referring to a court
- in-depth anti bullying staff training

The naivety of some social service staff is beyond belief. I have observed similar traits among housing associations, workplace HR's and school heads. This needs social research. It is clear professionals are often ill trained about the devious nature of bullies and how to recognise bullying. Information sharing is another lacuna. The Laming Report concluded that many abusive parents are manipulative and must not be automatically believed. Right of entry for social workers is vital. Days or even weeks are lost whilst getting permission from courts or police to enter properties and remove children or adults at risk. Social

Workers need the right to enter properties on suspicion of abuse with no waiting time. Likewise, Childline on hearing a child reporting abuse need professionals to investigate immediately. In the prevention of institutional abuse, there ought to be a mystery shopper system with covert inspectors visiting premises unannounced several times a year. If such simple measures were implemented it would make a huge difference, coupled with post-action statistical monitoring.

* * *

SPACE FOR YOUR NOTES:

11: BULLYING IN THE COMMUNITY

- who bullies whom
- likely victims
- types of bullying (anti-social behaviour)
- hate crime
- countering bully behaviour
- action for hate crime victims
- action by the authorities
- restorative justice
- THE ANTI-SOCIAL BEHAVIOUR CRIME & POLICING ACT 2014:
- NEW LEGAL MEASURES (a – i)
- COMMENT

Who bullies Whom

Bullying in the community is known as anti-social behaviour (ASB). Whilst some ASB is a criminal offence, there is no coverall law. But many distressing bully behaviours are addressed in the 2017 updates to the 2014 Anti-Social Behaviour Crime & Policing Act. This adds new measures and broadens existing laws. The Act is summarised at the end of this section with information from the excellent plain English guides (refer Resources/information).

So, who bullies whom? Meet classroom bully, older but no wiser having bullied family and colleagues and now creating havoc in the community. This is the depressing tale of the bully's progress. Hogarth would have found it interesting as a subject alongside his Rake's Progress and Harlot's Progress. In the community, bullies annoy tenants, home owners, shopkeepers, old people and nice people. There is a well-known phenomenon of group bullying of newcomers by long-standing neighbours, a hotbed for bigotry that is hopefully nearing the end of its time. An infamous example are the Brislington vigilantes (refer to Hate Crime, below).

Likely Victims

The usual targets; anyone perceived odd or different because of lifestyle choice, appearance, an unsexy disability, mental illness or simply being different. Groups are also likely to be targeted. Long-established communities can turn on newcomers (incomers) who have not yet learned its rules or kow-towed to self-appointed leaders. Newbies can be excluded, talked about, refused service in shops. This is all bully behaviour. Remember our maxim? Bullying is deliberate humiliation **or exclusion** by dint of a personal quality, looks, talent, skill or belief. Some long-term residents might be shocked being labelled bullies, but they need to know. Faith membership is enough to trigger bullying and has become a common excuse for harassing followers of Islam. If you live in a multi-racial city you know 90% of individuals from all races live peaceably until troublemakers/rumour mongers let loose. Thankfully, the Police Act provides remedies for discriminatory behaviour in the new criminal offence of Hate Crime.

In social housing estates, individuals tease victims for kicks. Those choosing to live unstimulating lives without ambition or will to improve are likely to remain in this grey psychological landscape. Housing Associations regularly update tenancy agreements, adding exceptions against new anti-social behaviours. Trash your surroundings, shout and scream, let your dog attack or foul, throw litter, hold drunken parties, leave rusting cars in the drive and you stand to lose your tenancy. Hurrah say other tenants, often after years of intimidation. Another issue is where social and private housing collide. This is happening more frequently now the law demands a certain percentage of social housing in every new build scheme.

Types of Bullying (anti-social behaviour)
Criminal ASB includes:

- harassment or intimidation
- anything that causes alarm or distress
- graffiti, littering, setting fire to rubbish
- damage to property
- excessive noise in unsocial hours or outside pubs
- drinking to excess or drug taking in public
- causing a nuisance or disturbance
- vigilante behaviour

It is difficult to catch bullies unless you have CCTV with night vision & motion sensors (otherwise you wade through 24/7 of video to catch miscreants). Harassments run from low grade but persistent pranks by 'adults' to riotous behaviour under the influence of drugs or alcohol.

Hate Crime
Hate Crime is 'hostility towards victim's disability, race, religion, sexual orientation or trans-gender identity,' (Crown Prosecution service description). These are known as protected characteristics and are the only example of direct anti bully legislation. Hate, as recognised by the Crown Prosecution Service, has many interpretations; unfriendliness, antagonism, resentment, dislike. The new law covers verbal abuse, intimidation, threats, harassment, assault, bullying and damage to property. An example is the horrific murder of disabled Iranian tenant, Bijan Ebrahimi in 2013. This man was subjected to abuse for 7 years, reporting 40 incidents which were largely ignored as he was falsely branded a liar. The ensuing enquiry criticised institutional racism in the police force and forged many procedural changes. Later four officers connected with the case were dismissed for

unprofessional behaviour and institutional racism. This recalls a similar case; the murder of Stephen Lawrence. His death drew negative comment about lack of support and institutional racism. Mr and Mrs Lawrence campaigned tirelessly and this bore fruit with changes to police procedures.

Countering Bully Behaviour
In her book, 'Bully Proof Kids', Brenda O'Malley says there is more cooperation in communities who depend on neighbours but less in wealthier places where people protect what they have. If you live in the north of Scotland in a community based on a product, this makes sense. So too if you live in crime-ridden parts of London where, shockingly, knife crime is higher than New York.

Wise local organisations encourage community initiatives such as Best Kept Village, city allotment schemes, charities providing low-cost loans for housing improvement, credit unions, sports schemes and schemes for young people like the Prince's Trust. It is not all about dealing with crime but encouraging communities to share in improving lives. Run by volunteers, their efforts help counter bully environments. Housing Associations encourage tenants to take part in competitions which encourage environmental improvement. They use anti-social behaviour teams to deal with disputes. Most HA's have a refuge or safe house where anyone who has been harassed or made anxious can stay up to a week for respite. Safe houses have a warden who offers a listening ear. Each guest has a room but there is a communal kitchen and lounge for those wanting to share experiences. Anyone with a mental health condition exacerbated by stress can use the facilities.

Action for Victims of Hate Crime

It is your civic duty to report ALL hate crime to the police, either in person or using the confidential online reporting system. Keep records; date, whom, incident, time and names of witnesses. Ask witnesses if they are willing to make a statement but do not be shocked or hurt if they refuse. Give their details to the police and leave intelligence-gathering to them. Many people will not want to be involved but do not take it personally. They may fear reprisals or being hectored in court by defence barristers. It takes great courage to appear as a defence witness.

If you are the target of harassment, catcalling or physical violence, carry a personal alarm (the police sometimes supply these). It would be useful to wear a small digital audio recording device which fits in a pocket. Learn to switch it on unobtrusively and fix the microphone in your shirt, blouse or jacket. Make sure no one sees it and do not tell anyone who might blab about it. At home, fit CCTV or a motion activated web cam preferably with cloud storage. Both can be bought cheaply at Argos, B&Q or online. There are also websites which offer free software for converting a web cam into recordable CCTV. Motion-activated equipment is best because you do not have to trawl through hours of footage to get to the incident. Another option for those with smart phones are hive cameras which send an email or live footage to your phone if there is an intruder. These cost £35 upwards plus call charges.

The thugs who perpetrate bullying will be expert in breaking and entering. If you reported hate crime, the police offer a free inspection by their security expert who will fit door locks, window locks and a hood to prevent thumb-lock latches being operated through the letter box. They recommend you lock all windows when you go out, hiding the keys but not forgetting to unlock when you are at home in case of fire. Even a small top window can be entered if left open. A security expert told me thugs do not care about hurting themselves and will dive through the smallest open windows. If you are experiencing abuse from a whole family it is likely they have 'trained' their kids to break and enter as well as harass, so locking windows is vital to exclude these mini Fagins.

If you see the perpetrator or their bully supports in the street, go to a public place where there are a lot of people such as a library or pub. Never run but walk confidently. Do not respond to taunts or turn around to argue. If you are in a residential street, knock the nearest door and ask if they will let you shelter and call the police. If you see your tormentors on a lonely road, thumb a lift from a car, bus or taxi. Public transport bosses are beginning to accept this might happen and are beginning to cooperate.

Remove your private details from websites especially social media like Facebook. Do not publicise your date of birth, postcode, school address or work address. If you have delete them. If you suspect your computer has been hacked change ALL passwords and email addresses. Block offenders from sites you want to re-visit. And remember, if someone does access your computer it is extremely difficult to completely delete material. The police have trace experts to deal with such instances.

Do not let this taint your life. Deal with one day at a time. Continue socializing but be sensible. Never walk home alone whether male or female. Do not give up hobbies, skills and talents but focus on them. Keep a positives diary where you record good things every day. There will always be something to record even if it is that you have been gifted another day of life. Start each day with confidence. Implement ideas from the Empowerment section. Breathing exercises and mindfulness are good for living in the moment. Get professional and peer support from counselling, mediation or an online anti bully support group. If you are young, contact Childline or a teacher. Teachers can help even if the bullying is not at school. For young adults, join a youth club or somewhere you will be with like-minded peers. This will boost your confidence and reduce isolation.

Action by the Authorities

The new law allows the authorities rapid response to miscreant behaviour, with on-the-spot fines, injunctions, statutory notices, confiscation powers and the ability to close public areas without court application. There is a great deal of ASB not classed as criminal but still a nuisance. Neighbour disputes spoil the peace in communities, often misunderstandings that escalate. Even issues that start small must be dealt with quickly or it can get out of hand, as it did in Brislington.

Restorative justice

This is an alternative to a fine or prison sentence in civil and criminal cases. It has to have the consent of victim and perpetrator. The victim talks to a restorative justice professional and decides if they wish to meet the perpetrator, face to face or at a distance (teleconferencing). Victim and perpetrator meet at a restorative justice conference with a police officer. The victim has an opportunity to tell the perpetrator how they felt as a result of the behaviour. The aim is to gain apology and closure.

THE ANTI-SOCIAL BEHAVIOUR, CRIME & POLICING ACT 2014

Recent updates to this Act are far reaching, encompassing and updating existing laws with devolved discretionary powers for police, Housing Associations and Local Authorities. As this book is primarily about bullying, I will mention only those parts which come under this heading. Although bullying is not yet classed as criminal, bully behaviour is covered by other laws. The following brief notes are about sections of the new Act:

* summary & intention of the Act
* bullying
* Intimidating group behaviour
* littering
* noise nuisance
* THE NEW LEGAL MEASURES

Summary & Intention of the Act

The Act is about the protection of victims rather than punishment of offenders and gives authorities far more wide-ranging powers. Rather than fixing punishments, they have discretion how to act. The victim in some cases can choose the perpetrator's punishment, for example mediation, on-the-spot fines or restorative justice. It is these discretionary powers which go a long way toward ensuring closure for victims. As well as the sections I have summarised the Act covers other community crimes:

* protection for victims of forced marriages
* female genital mutilation
* drug taking in public places
* to confiscate objects used to intimidate – objects used as weapons
* improved port and border security

Schools are obliged by law to provide anti bullying measures, including anti bully training. The Department of Education offers guidelines which are heavily slanted toward prevention. Teachers and Heads have wider powers to deal with bully pupils both in school and in the community. The new IPNA (injunction to prevent nuisance) allows miscreants to be apprehended and forbidden to enter certain areas, made to take anti bullying training and given compulsory counselling or mentoring. Bully behaviour is legislated through:

1. The Protection from Harassment Act 1997
2. Malicious Communications Act 2003
3. Public Order Act 1986
4. Sections 90 & 91. The Education & Inspections Act
5. The Public Protection Order
6. Section 88, The Environmental Protection Act

Harassment & Intimidation

This section covers victims of targeted behaviour such as:

- neighbours annoying guests & visitors of the victim
- loud, drunken parties
- aggressive or nuisance conduct by individuals

Perpetrators can be given an IPNA Injunction without a court order. This bans them from getting within a certain distance of the person they annoyed. There is the possibility of a Criminal Behaviour Order or prosecution under the Protection from Harassment Act 1997. As well as powers of arrest the authority can issue temporary banning orders or close a public place, alley or park where ASB took place.

Intimidating Group Behaviour

Many householders report feeling fearful when confronted with groups of youths drinking or drug taking in town centres. Time was when a female could not walk through a city centre without being accosted or propositioned. The law recognises youths en masse do not always pose a threat and try to balance human rights whilst preventing bad behaviour. A case in point is graffiti inciting hate crimes, as against graffiti as art. Banksy's graffiti is often encouraged in Bristol because of its high value. The new law outlines criminal offences of varying scale:

- damage to property, including graffiti and vandalism
- noise nuisance, particularly in unsocial hours
- threatening or aggressive behaviour
- littering (private & public property)
- drunkenness in public

The police can disperse groups if the behaviour is harassing passers-by and close the area permanently or temporarily. The Public Protection Order allows them to ban certain behaviours in the problem area. Whilst this applies to nuisance behaviour, the Government recognises the balance between bans on nuisance makers and the human rights of law-abiding homeless people, demonstrators and campaigners.

Littering
Littering has long been a problem for example dustbins emptied over property after petty arguments. Nuisance littering is now dealt with by a Local Authority through acceptable behaviour contracts, mediation or warning letters. A Local Authority can issue a Community Protection Notice (CPN) for persistent littering or accumulating waste, a measure to prevent hoarders spoiling the lives of neighbours. Councils can clear rubbish without the owner's consent and issue a statutory nuisance notice if the litter is an environmental hazard. Littering and dumping in public places is on the agenda of the new Act. Dumping is an expensive nuisance with Local Authorities spending thousands of pounds clearing illegal waste. Section 88 of the Environmental Protection Act allows fixed penalty notices or spot fines for miscreants who dump rubbish.

Noise Nuisance

Good news for those subjected to noise nuisance from loud parties, a constant bass beat from a boom box or over-loud machinery. The new Act covers unreasonable tenant noise. What is not covered is noise due to poor building design or lifestyle choice. Housing Associations might offer sound deadening boards or infill if the cost is not prohibitive. The test for application of the law is if the noise breaches, 'interference with personal comfort or amenity of neighbours or the nearby community.' A Local Authority, Housing Association or police can intervene. The Local Authority can fit sound recording equipment and confiscate offending equipment on the spot.

NEW LEGAL MEASURES (A–I)

The new powers offer rapid relief from nuisance and are backed by legislative powers (see above). Each behaviour has a test; the condition[s] under which the law applies. Measures can be enforced through more than one agency, giving delegated power to Housing Associations and Local Authorities. Miscreants can be dealt with on the spot with punitive legal measures if they refuse to comply.

a. **Community Trigger**. If after reporting ASB for six months there is no outcome a victim can appeal for a Case Review (Community Trigger). Every statement, investigation and piece of evidence is re-examined by a senior official. To start the process write to the local Anti-Social Behaviour Co-ordinator, call 101 or complete an online form on your police website. The coordinator provides a written report stating whether anything can be done or if the case must be closed due to lack of evidence. Hard evidence is difficult to obtain unless you have 24/7 CCTV and personal recording devices. Hardened miscreants are likely to take precautions like wearing gloves or carrying out their behaviour on different days at different times. However, one day they will trip up. Police files contain anecdotal evidence of incredible stupidity with petty criminals leave traces on victim's food, divots of mud on doormats, smears of blood, personal clothing or jewellery left in burgled property. In one report, the miscreant having drunk the victim's beer was found asleep in the victim's bed by the police. Housing Associations have a small stock of CCTV which is used as a rule to gather evidence for domestic violence. They will sometimes loan CCTV to victims of persistent anti social behaviour.

b. **Community Remedy.** This allows victims to have a say in the punishment of a perpetrator of anti-social behaviour. It is for low-level offences like minor damage, graffiti or dog nuisance. A community resolution or youth conditional caution is usually issued. These are the kind of punishments victims can choose for perpetrators:

- writing a letter of apology to the victim
- cleaning up graffiti
- paying for damage
- litter picking or picking up dog's mess
- being made to sign an acceptable behaviour contract
- attend a course, e.g. alcoholics anonymous, anger management, dog training

This goes some way in giving victims closure after enduring extensive anti social behaviour.

c. **Civil Injunction.** These are more serious and are issued by County or High Court for over 18's, Youth Courts for under 18's:

- large scale graffiti
- large scale littering

- large scale waste or dumping
- bullying
- dog issues, including attack
- drug taking
- abuse of alcohol in public
- noise nuisance

Many agencies can now issue punishments; Local Authorities, Housing Associations, Chief Officer of Police, Chief Constable of Transport Police, Environment Agency and NHS Protect. They can order an unlimited fine, 2 years imprisonment to over 18's, supervision order for under 18's, civil detention order for up to 3 months. The test for the law is if it has caused harassment, alarm or distress, annoyance to the complainant's residential premises. These orders also apply to visitors of the perpetrator if they commit an offence; closure of another loop hole.

d. **Criminal Behaviour Order.** This allows an order via the Crown Prosecution Service for threats or acts of violence OR 'causing alarm, harassment or distress' to individuals or groups. Breaching is a criminal offence and the miscreant liable to a hefty fine or 3 months imprisonment for over 18's. If objects or weapons are used, these can be confiscated and the wrongdoer must leave the area for up to 48 hours. These measures can be accessed by police or community support officers.

e. **Dispersal Power.** This applies to anyone age over 10 and allows for dispersal of groups who harass or distress residents or passers-by. They must leave the area for at least 48 hours and any items used in the breach are confiscated, weapons or otherwise. There is a fine or 3 months imprisonment for over 18's who refuse to comply. This action is limited to police or community support officers.

f. **Community Protection Notice**. This provides multiple agencies the right to 'stop persons 16 and over committing ASB which spoils the community's quality of life;' littering, hoarding, animal-related issues, action causing vermin or effluvia, making excessive or unreasonable noise. This notice can be issued by Police Community Support Officers (PCSO), Housing Associations or Local Authorities. Breaches are dealt with through written warning, fixed penalty or imprisonment.

g. **Public Places Protection Order** (PSPO). This allows anyone to be removed from a public place, park, alley or communal area and the place closed if there is 'persistent and unreasonable behaviour.' The order allows for temporary or permanent closure up to three years, for example if the site is being used for drug taking or alcohol abuse. It can be used in the case of dog attacks, fouling or groups annoying passers-by. Defaulters are issued with a fixed penalty notice.

h. **Closure Power**. This can be used by Local Authorities and the police where nuisance, public disorder or criminal activity is committed in a public place. They can close the area for 48 hours, then 3 further months by order of a Magistrate's Court. Breaching is subject to 3 – 6 months of imprisonment.

i. **Absolute Ground for Possession**. Housing Associations and private landlords can apply for immediate re-possession. The tenant must have breached the law, an injunction, displayed criminal behaviour, caused excessive noise or had a civil ASBO order (these must have been previously proven in court).

COMMENT
The Police Act offers rapid relief for harassed tenants and passers-by. The fact that many agencies can implement the

law without waiting for the police allows speedy resolution. Multiple laws and statutes are brought under one system, allowing greater flexibility when deciding which law applies; another loophole closed. As the Government says, citizens have a duty to help uphold the law, to report offenders and ensure everyone is protected from harassment and harm.

In researching this book, my experience of being bullied and my professional knowledge, there are measures which could usefully be implemented. This is my wish list:

My Wish List:

1. A countrywide network of welcome centres run by charities and volunteers for newcomers. These might be linked with CAB, Age Concern, charity shops and mental health charities. The centres would provide a welcome pamphlet for newcomers with community activities as well as a page with emergency contacts.

2. Training in anti bullying measures for staff and volunteers of all help agencies and major charities.

3. provision of loan CCTV / audio recording devices for social housing tenants or private homeowners who cannot afford equipment. This would be subject to deposit and agreement to return equipment, enforceable through the National Insurance office.

4. A safe place on every estate where someone in danger can be given shelter and the police called. This could be a warden's house, estate office, local 24 hour shop or private houses of known volunteers.

5. An agreed hand signal (sign language) used by anyone being chased by hate crime offenders in lonely spots at night for public transport to stop and offer shelter.

6. induction for tenants to include anti bullying information and

warnings about measures for breaches. Offer free lunch to bring them flocking!

7. mediation compulsory for perpetrators of anti-social behaviour. Those who refuse to receive a written notice that if acts are repeated and mediation refused they will risk losing the tenancy.
8. Make it illegal for defence Barristers to hector witnesses or ruin the credibility of experts. This is a huge problem and why witnesses are reluctant to appear in court.
9. Those with no legal help in civil cases provided with pro bono barrister, as is current practice in criminal courts.

* * *

SPACE FOR YOUR NOTES:

12: FROM BYSTANDER TO UPSTANDER

'The only thing necessary for the triumph of evil is that good men do nothing.' attributed to Edmund Burke, 18th century Politician.

'90% of bullying is witnessed by those who do nothing. The more people present, the less likely someone will help,' Stella O'Malley [refer diagram, Group Behaviour].

Video on YouTube: *An elderly woman shopper sees thieves on motor scooters smashing the windows of a jewellery shop. As terrified staff close the shutters, the woman runs half the length of the street and begins whirling her handbag at one of the thieves. Onlookers comment but do nothing. When a thief throws a punch at the woman, an onlooker shouts, 'he's attacking the old lady' and several youths intervene. They apprehend the attacker as his accomplices escape.*

Amazing things can be accomplished by bystanders. In the case above, one woman's bravery triggered acts of solidarity and the villains were apprehended by ordinary citizens who became upstanders. It could have gone the other way – that lady might have been killed. From bystander to upstander is a step that frequently does not happen. Why? Cultural embarrassment, the 'not me' syndrome, insecurity (fearing consequences)? Remember little Madeleine McCann? Years later a couple thought they recognised her and snatched a young girl who appeared distressed. It was, sadly, not Madeleine – but might have been. They did the right thing. It takes courage to do something despite fear of looking a fool. Would you do it?

These are rules of thumb for bystanders:

1. do not minimise bullying or its effects
2. do not encourage social acceptance of bystanding

3. never give useless advice e.g. 'ignore it', 'be strong', 'get over it'
4. teach people that bullies love an audience and bystanders feed this need
5. a bystander can tell a bully their behaviour is not acceptable
6. bystanders in schools can be encouraged to become anti bully ambassadors
7. teach bystanders about group behaviour – e.g. YouTube video above
8. a bystander can engage a victim in benign conversation i.e. show a bully this person is not an outsider
9. to be neutral is as much a crime as being a bully
10. if you see a hate message online, post a positive message
11. help other bystanders realize their hidden power to change things
12. taking into account appropriate fear (e.g. sociopaths or weapon-wielding bullies), never shirk from dealing with injustice;
13. if you cannot deal with it, report it

* * *

SPACE FOR YOUR NOTES:

13: BULLY TO LEADER

Some bullies are doomed to remain as they are. They are likely to become hardened criminals spending years in prison or embittered solitaries with a grudge against everyone and everything or a wandering mercenary beloved by no one.

Bullies often have strengths that can be trained; they are strong-minded and can persuade others to a cause. Think Henry V's speech before Agincourt; this would not have worked if Henry was mild-mannered. Doggedness is useful if the bully is willing to learn but to do so needs education; to be taught group dynamics, that society needs variety to thrive and moral behaviour brings its own rewards. Bully supports must be brought in too; a reformed bully is capable of changing minds if they dedicate an obstinate nature instead of using this to torment victims. The challenge is how to motive those with short triggers and excessive energy.

Stella O'Malley offers great ideas for reforming school bullies. She suggests teachers get them to write on subjects connected with loyalty and compassion. Also, to encourage a better view of intellectual or creative victims, by giving the whole school a day off if someone achieves academically or in the creative arts. She writes of a time Irish sports fans lived up to a good reputation by engaging in good-natured banter, rather than aggravating rival fans. Everyone is motivated by being commended instead of demonized and we all like unexpected treats. Bullies are no different.

Psychology is a powerful tool for positive change used in the right direction. We need to use it in reclaiming bullies to 'the useful and the good' (as Tennyson writes in his powerful poem, Ulysses). We need to point out role models like Bear Grylls, who displays his strength in appropriate circumstances yet is highly moral with a strong sense of decency and community. Bear is

Diagram 3:   BULLY TO LEADER

(based on Stella O'Malley, 'Bully Proof Kids')

- **a bully** has the capacity to become a leader if they find a mentor (role model).
- a strong personality with the ability to recruit is a trait of leadership.
- **a victim** can become a leader if they become more assertive.

victim & bully are able to learn to see both sides of the issues – if they choose to.

- dominate / intimidate
- use information as powe
- fear new ideas
- cant take dissent
- low expectations
- immature
- deny faults

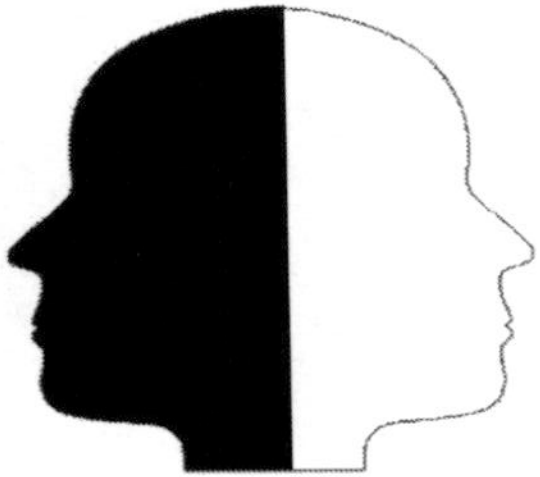

- lead by example
- share information
- welcome new opinions
- encourage individuals
- emotionally intelligent
- admit faults
- emotionally mature

113

more Alexander the Great than Attila the Hun yet a respected soldier and former member of the elite SAS.

A a leader is different from a tyrant. And whereas every tyrant eventually falls, like Ozymandias in Shelley's poem, good leaders are remembered. It is in the interest of communities to help steer bullies towards a role that keeps them occupied and gives them a sense of achievement. The devil makes mischief for idle hands!

* * *

SPACE FOR YOUR NOTES:

14: ON & UP: COMMUNITY SUPPORT

Today's society is more fragmented than throughout history. There is little full time work, leading to families separated during the week. The breadwinner rents a small property near work, often far from the family home, where there is little sense of belonging. This leads to lack of support from families, putting strain on relationships. Remarriage often brings children from a former marriage who have to be brought up on limited income. The fruit of such fragmentation is isolation, anxiety, little sense of belonging, lack of culture and identity. These bonding gaps used to be filled by religion. The nearest replacements are national events like royal weddings, sports, social media and terrorism. But as yet no one has discovered a universal panacea.

Without a bonding factor, it is no surprise to sociologists that disillusioned youth turn to crime, knife crime, alcohol & drug taking, gang membership or terrorism. If you like, these are faiths they would not espouse except for lack of cohesion and identity. This lack of belonging is as dangerous to modern man as being alone would be to a primitive man. This was brought home in a BBC4 documentary, 'Civilisations Under Attack' where historian Dan Cruickshank asked a terrorist the reasons for his destructive behaviour. He received no coherent answer apart from inane grinning by the interviewee, clearly loving his time in the limelight. Imams despair at their faith hi-jacked; the so-called jihads (holy war) against innocent civilians world-wide. This is not genuine faith but a form of bullying.

The only way to tackle these issues is to develop the mindset of Mother Theresa; give relief to one person at a time. Cumulative measures also 'drip-drip' a difference over time. These are some old and new ideas towards a better society;

- citizenship education at primary school level
- teaching in primary school on anti bullying
- family education – not limited to deprived areas
- bully to leader courses in schools and prisons
- encouraging creative as well as academic excellence in schools
- re-purposing of destructive behaviour
- punitive measures for those who do not conform
- anti-social legislation – e.g. the new police act
- devolved legal powers for social & community workers
- extra monitoring of problem families
- prison reform
- free cctv loan for social hotspots
- use of government mystery shoppers for institutions
- awards like the Duke of Edinburgh scheme, but for adults
- pride in community awards targeted at marginalised groups
- more disability awareness, e.g. BBC using disabled presenters

SUMMARY

Bullying does not happen in isolation. It cannot continue without bully supports; individuals who condone/join in, bystanders who fail to act. Happily morality is slowly entering the consciousness of the wider public, with an increasing number of Internet forums to voice protests (refer to Resources). It is vital all helpers, upstanders, legislators, school Heads, HR departments and campaigners learn these areas:

- roles of the major players in bully environments
- how bullying affects ALL the major players
- human group dynamics (group behaviour)
- how bullying escalates (toxic environments)
- physical and mental signs of stress (distress)
- how stress affects thinking, behaviour and action

- bully prevention techniques for each environment
- how to support victims
- how to deal with bullies AND help them reform

All the above are contained in this book, together with further reading, help organisations, websites and anti bullying forums. It is vital the victim gets support and is encouraged to continue their day-to-day activity. Above all, help squash the myth that victims are weak. It is better to focus on discovering why this happened and how it can be prevented. Attitude formations are not helpful, neither is hijacking situations by individuals playing good girl/boy to resolve situations for reward (*Berne called this stroking*) which leads to blaming and scapegoating. There is no excuse in this age of communication for anyone to live in fear without hope of relief.

* * *

SPACE FOR YOUR NOTES:

LEVEL 2: MORE ABOUT THE MAJOR PLAYERS

15: THE VICTIM (TARGET)

- characteristics of victims
- large scale bullying – 2 examples
- 'why me?'
- VICTIM EXPERIENCES & TRAITS
- why do victims develop these traits?
- victimhood and false victims
- victims in recovery
- crossovers

Characteristics of Victims

A persistent but untruthful urban myth is that victims are weak or bullied because they do not 'act strong' or 'ignore' bully behaviour. Clearly these myth-makers never experienced bullying, let alone relentless persecution by a sociopath or sociopathic family. Victims (targets) are either chosen for a particular trait the bully /bullies envy or were selected as scapegoats because they are perceived to represent something the group or clique dislike. The following are recognised victim traits (though not every victim fits these patterns):

- have attributes a bully envies. character, skills, talents, many friendships, success
- or unsociable, isolated, marginalised (autism, sensory disorder, disability, loner)
- lack confidence or will lack confidence after extensive/ prolonged bullying

- are different to the bully clique – physically, behaviour, looks, values
- may show visible signs of anxiety or shyness; behavioural traits
- innovate ideas which the bully group fear / refuse to accept
- may have been abused as children and 'expect' to be abused
- perceived as 'fair game' because their group appear to reject them
- may deny they are being bullied
- can be self-negating and refuse help
- hope bullying will cease spontaneously
- can be passive or highly emotional (creative temperament)

Large Scale Bullying – 2 examples

As we know, the infamous extermination of Jews in Nazi Germany marked a particularly horrific part of the Second World War. Hitler came to power in the 1930's at a time when Germany was economically unsound. He had been brought up in Vienna where the Mayor was a Jew-hater and hatred of Jews was commonplace world wide. This was typified in the 17th century by the character Shylock in 'The Merchant of Venice,' whom Shakespeare portrayed as a rich, greedy moneylender. A false 19th century science called Eugenics was popular in Hitler's time. This advocated Aryans (blonde Germanic types) as the superior race and claimed other races intermarrying would weaken the Aryan line. Morel, a psychologist, published a paper on degeneracy in families which appeared to support this false hypothesis. Hitler was a firm believer in Eugenics and when he came to power, popularised himself by demonising Jews. He claimed eliminating Jews would have two effects; improving the economy thus ensuring the future of the 'pure' Aryan bloodline (see diagram 4 overleaf).

Hitler's 'solution' was swallowed wholesale by stressed, cash-strapped Germans who only discovered their folly once the

Diagram 4 – KEY PLAYERS:
motives & interactions

Roles interchange: see arrows. Each has many 'types' – lower case
Examples: victim to bully or rescuer; bully to victim or bully support.
floater to winning side or bully or bystander.

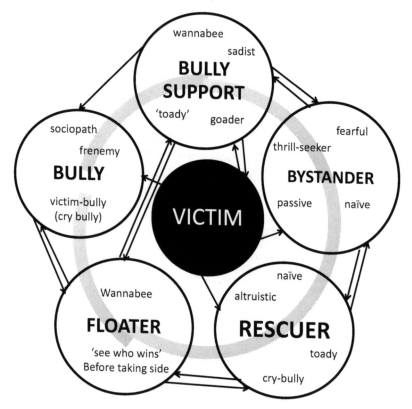

Jews had been practically annihilated. To this day the Germans are ashamed of what went on yet they were by no means the only ones to remain bystanders. Jews persecuted by Nazis had once been bankers, successful business people, doctors, artists, very pious individuals, decent working people, before being scapegoated ostensibly for Germany's financial and social problems.

A second example is the Salem Witch Trials of 1692. This time was unsettled, with native Americans at war with new settlers and tensions between poorer and richer communities in the area. When a group of young girls claimed to have been possessed by the devil, a small group of older women were blamed, women already marginalised by that society. Trials were held during which other 'victims' appeared; hallucinating, foaming at the mouth and fitting. 19 people were eventually hanged and an estimated 200 brought to trial on the basis of these dubious symptoms, which have been recently conjectured to be caused by ergot poisoning, if not gross imagination. The story became infamous because the trials were based on hearsay without a scrap of evidence other than hysterical girls.

It is vital to understand the above process because it also applies to individuals:

1. victim[s] targeted by bully (*varying reasons*)
2. targeted programme of ridicule/hate crime against victim[s] by bully
3. bully persuades others to join in (*i.e. they become bully supports*)
4. victim[s] loses dignity (humanity) in the eyes of group
5. scapegoating (*victimization*) as others join in (*for their own reasons*)
6. group lose insight into their actions – victimisation is normalised

This pattern is commonplace in toxic environments, particularly the workplace. Whistleblower Law was introduced to help redress such situations.

Bullying sometimes ends with the death of victims. Victims of gang warfare and domestic violence frequently hit headlines. Many child deaths have been attributed to bullycide, where victims commit suicide after prolonged bullying. More often, the victim will leave the environment to try their luck elsewhere. This is the best strategy if the bully culture is deep rooted because remaining will almost certainly lead to long term psychological problems with reduced self confidence and self esteem.

'Why Me?'

This is frequently asked by targets. A victim or target is NOT responsible for inciting bullying, any more than a victim of rape 'invites' rape by what they do or how they appear. Victims happen to be in the wrong place at the wrong time. As the Bob Dylan song goes, 'you just happened to be there, that's all'. Sadly this blame myth sticks despite the efforts of change agencies. By definition a neuro-typical bully (one without mental illness or personality disorder) targets someone who appears to them more gifted, talented, attractive, wealthy (etc.); whatever trait particularly irks them. Conversely, victims often give up talents and skills hoping the bully will leave them alone. But they don't. Another major reason for victim targeting is the victim representing a cause or issue the bully/bullies dislike for example a religious doctrine, belief, idea, mode of dress or behaviour. The bully lacks confidence and finds it impossible to accept people who are different to them.

Bullies pick victims because they want to remove suffering from their shoulders and site it on someone else. Bullies lack empathy and are low on understanding. For sociopaths, anyone is a potential victim. All bullies show traits of the sociopath but unlike a personality disordered sociopath bullies can reform. The bully seeks easy victims; nice people who will not fight back and are reluctant to 'report' the bullying.

VICTIM EXPERIENCES & TRAITS

Wavering Emotional States

Victims go through a gamut of emotions. Though bullying like any loss is said to have stages, emotions of victims vary in type, order and duration. Victims might experience a mix of despair, fear, a reduced sense of self, frustration, helplessness, anger, denial and acceptance. These may be interspersed with bursts of rage often accompanied by murderous thoughts the strength of which may shock the victim and their loved ones. Extreme stress might make murderers of us all. There are many reports of victims of domestic violence who murder a partner after years of abuse, whether or not alcohol or drug fuelled. Conversely many victims refuse to leave a partner, particularly one who asks forgiveness each time, claiming they will mend their ways. The ups and downs of these relationships will drain the victim of will and energy over time. Some psychologists claim there is co-dependency between victims and bullies; one seeking power, the other wanting to remain child-like and helpless. This co dependency is often the result of childhood abuse of both victim and bully. Victims tend towards the 'glass half empty' view if bullying is continuous.

Lack of Confidence

Watch Carrie, the film based on Stephen King's book of the same name. It is a horror movie but makes the point about a victim finding her power. King based Carrie on a pupil at a school where he taught, a girl who was relentlessly persecuted until she committed suicide. The fictional Carrie fought back with devastating results.

Confidence ebbs and flows. Hormonal dips and surges, grief, loss, relationship problems, job loss, a cutting comment (meant or not), even seemingly positive things like marrying or moving house can all erode confidence.

Suspicion and Distrust

Being bullied results in mistrust but the reverse is also true. Those who distrust others are likely to become targets. Distrust comes from inside. You question yourself, your motives and the motives of others. You cannot accept compliments, gifts or invitations without asking why, as if you are not worthy. These are victim traits. Even a skilled and talented individual can distrust themselves and others. Suspicion is an isolating characteristic. The bully spots this and slowly erodes the victim's confidence by encouraging or coercing others to join in. It is a cycle seemingly impossible to break – but it can be.

Low Mood and Clinical Depression

Some individuals are prone to a medical condition called depressive illness which (in the medical model) is caused by lack of serotonin, one of the chemical mood enhancers produced in the brain. Low mood (triggered by loss, bereavement or negative life events) reduces production of serotonin. There are individuals born with little serotonin in their DNA and they will always be prone to low mood. Depressive illness is treated with ante-depressants which mimic and stimulate serotonin production. Although these lead to rapid relief, the patient must remain on medication until the brain produces its own serotonin. A GP or Psychiatrist judge when this is and that is why ante-depressants must be withdrawn under medical supervision. Low mood can be also triggered by lack of sunlight, a condition known as Seasonal Affective Disorder (or SAD). SAD is treated by using a light box in the winter months.

Not Fighting Back

Bullies choose victims who do not fight back. How do they know? A period of observation by the bully starts before bullying begins, which can take several months (often referred to as 'the honeymoon period'). There are many reasons victims fail to fight back. Religious reasons, wanting to appear nice, hating fuss or hoping the bullying will stop on its own.

Flashman types (aggressive, violent sociopaths) are best dealt with by professionals and use of covert webcams or CCTV for evidence. This is one occasion on which it is never a good idea to fight back but to walk away from the situation.

Shy /Isolated /Self Contained

Autistic, creative, intellectual types are commonly targeted by bullies. In schools, offices or a community, anyone who appears different to an in-crowd is a likely target. A bully wants a target they know is likely to be excluded, by judicious use of malicious gossip or covert threats. They rarely pick on someone they know will incite empathy.

Class Clown

Class clown is not a good mask to adopt for the prevention of bullying. Class clowns laugh at themselves in self defence, hoping to deflect put downs. This is a victim attitude. Some stand-up comics' patter includes derogatory material about their hang-ups, whether weight, appearance, belief or a disability. If it does not concern the person and earns them a living that might seem ok but it prolongs the myth about class clown being funny. In the classroom, clowns are not admired but despised.

Low Self Value

Negative childhood experience, not necessarily family abuse (though this is a causal factor) easily turns into lack of self belief. If most people around you offer strokes and kind words, your confidence will radiate. If they constantly nag and pick, the result is a reduced self worth. As I wrote previously, everyone lacks confidence occasionally, but this can lead to self reflection which promulgates growth and change. Many successful people launched careers after years of self doubt and make good role models for victims.

View Life as 'Glass Half Empty'

Lack of esteem colours life in gray. A haze of negativity can be spotted like a fog by a bully. Head down, rarely smiling, anxious when they enter a room, shy or insecure individuals are very visible to others though they do not realize this. Both a very confident and very nervous person are far more visible. A glass half empty person perceives the negative. Given a gift, they wonder why they deserve it, are suspicious as to why it has been given and may embarrass the giver by refusing it. By gifts I mean compliments too. Given an award they will claim they do not deserve it or it should have gone to someone else. Unlike Hollywood Oscar winners being emotionally generous, these individuals really mean they do not deserve it. They infuriate friends and relations by not accepting the smallest compliment, often leading these people to give up. This is self fulfilling prophesy; as compliments fade out, the glass-half-empty individual says, 'I knew it wouldn't last.' They believe they have done something to rile the bully and that they are responsible and deserve it. It is difficult to deal with. Everything will be twisted to the negative leaving any helper exhausted and frustrated. The victim will see this as more rejection.

Shy and Hiding

The sociophobe is a sitting target for bullies. Though socio-phobes accept compliments from friends and family they keep out the limelight and bullies notice this, homing in. Lack of sociability offers few opportunities to hone social skills and learn to deal with bullies and other difficult characters. Sociophobes do not regularly access simple acts that give confidence to others; thanks, compliments, a listening ear, encouragement, acts of kindness or generosity that many take for granted. Socialising with like-minded others is vital. It does not necessarily mean parties and social gatherings but feeling a part of the community and meeting others of like mind. Shy people and sociophobes benefit from volunteering where their effort will be appreciated even without being said – which is often more acceptable to them.

Why Do Victims Develop Such Traits?

There are may reasons victims develop these traits apart from genetic bad luck. Many live with dysfunctional families or have suffered abuse which colours how they perceive the world. Sometimes it is to do with DNA. Pioneers cope with and enjoy large amounts of solitariness but loneliness is different. Lone-liness means you feel no one cares and that makes a difference to how you might be treated by bullies and everyone else. It is a sad fact that isolated individuals are unpopular. Their anxiety and gloom are off-putting. They are difficult to encourage. They become hypersensitive to hurt, seeing it where it is not meant. Always at the edge of life they want to join in but often don't know how. They might appear snobbish or stand-offish but this is an outside perspective. Inside they are often desperate to find a friend. This desperation is likely to attract power-hungry sociopaths and narcissists always ready to find their next victim.

Children already traumatized are more likely to be bullied at school. They are more likely to become prey of unsavoury characters who roam like hungry wolves at the edge of every community, as they do at refugee camps and famine feeding stations throughout the world. In this respect life is neither fair nor just.

Victimhood and False Victims

The doubled-edged term victimhood is why therapists prefer the word target instead of victim, when describing someone who has been bullied. Psychologists claim the process of victim-hood increases the vulnerability of targets who never learn to defend themselves (always expecting rescue). Also a victim remains 'down' because they do not have to take up challenges or risk change. Like a beaten dog they lick the hand that beats them, for this is the only love they expect to receive.

The other side of victimhood is false victims; attention seekers lured by the glamour if the cause is popular or subject of a moral panic. This hijacking is for personal glory. In psychological terms they project (get rid of) negative feelings on a well-known cause, claiming to be victims of it and falsely claiming to believe in it. This century has seen increasing numbers of urban terrorists murdering under the cloak of religious war (jihad) or centuries-old disputes long forgotten by reasonable folk. Asked to explain their cause, as did historian Dan Cruikshank, they fail, proving their espousal a sham. Why do they do this? Not only does their frustration disappear they can delude themselves they are right

LEVEL 2: MORE ABOUT THE MAJOR PLAYERS

minded. They fail to see their targets as human, like Nazis and witch hunters, yet first to complain when badly treated. Rose West (serial killer) murdered her daughter yet complained when fellow prisoners killed her pet hamster.

In the personality disorder Munchhausen Syndrome By Proxy, a perpetrator harms a child (theirs or someone they are looking after) then pretends to be rescuer. A mother poisons her child then attends hospital, enjoying attention as 'anxious mother of injured child'. An au pair wounds her charge then calls an ambulance claiming the child had an accident, enjoying the rescuer role. These are false victims, the real victim being the child who becomes very ill or dies.

A sign of increasing media attention to victimhood is the tendency of TV or radio stations to offer help lines after broadcasting material emotionally sensitive material. A caption, 'trigger [*then the subject matter*]' is displayed before such programmes, warning viewers they might be affected by what follows. Whether this is genuine caring or an attempt to avoid being sued is debatable but this points to victimisation that is perhaps over the top. Human rights are vital but allowing false victims to rule brings its own dangers.

Victims in Recovery
According to urban myth, victims are helpless, blameworthy, weak, deserving being bullied for not 'fighting back'. But in recovery victims become angry which is a positive trait. Anger is a dynamic force for change. Those who overcome bullying become enthusiastic learners, empathic, resilient and ambitious. Therapists always encourage victims to pursue goals. Bullies who attend for therapy are encouraged to discover suitable goals rather than envy the achievements of others. Reformed bullies make good leaders using the same traits that once lead them

astray. Looked at this way, you might accept how a bully is also a victim, in a way.

CROSSOVERS

Unsurprisingly, victims can become bullies. Frustrated with being abused they turn on those weaker than themselves. The mother who has been abused as a child raises her hand to her sleeping baby. The bullied sibling becomes school bully or office tyrant or one person crime wave. The victim becomes bully manager. The marginalised schoolboy becomes tyrant politician or leader. But equally a bullied child can turn altruistic; a campaigner, an upstander who intervenes. With strong feelings they are unlikely to be floaters but fit the strong role of rescuer.

* * *

SPACE FOR YOUR NOTES:

130

16: THE BULLY

- nature of a bully
- the fatal gene
- child abuse to bully adult
- need for power & control
- low self esteem
- envy & greed
- revenge & spite
- crossover roles
- whom do they target?

'There are two kinds of people in the world. The first look at others who have accomplished things and thinks, 'why them? Why not me?' The other looks at those same people and thinks, 'If they can do it, why can't I?'

'The Daily Stoic', Ryan Holiday.

Nature of a Bully

In the first part of the epigram above, Ryan Holiday neatly encapsulates the ethos of bullies. There are two types of bully. The first and less commonplace is someone with a personality disorder (e.g. sociopath and narcissist).The second is someone who bullies in given circumstances. This book is mainly about the second category though I offer a brief outline of the other type in the next section. Bullies-by-circumstance can reform if they choose to do so and accept an opportunity. Sometimes this opportunity occurs forcibly, as the result of a prison sentence. There is no bully who has never had an opportunity to change, though they might not be ready or recognise an opportunity has been given. Sometimes an opportunity has to be pointed out to them by an upstander or professional who has observed their behaviour.

Bullies are cowardly, surrounded by cronies, would-be bullies, covert supporters and fearful floaters. A bully might suck up to authority but will not associate with anyone they consider weak. For weak read thoughtful, uncomplaining, unassuming or shy. Bullies like to be admired and feared. They do not like rivals who have an eye on their bully role. Such persons will quickly be ejected from the group (gang, clique, family). For bullies quantity counts over quality. They don't care about others needs, beliefs or circumstances; they want everyone to serve them. When the bully meets a new recruit there might be a show of concern at first but this will be a ploy to gather information. It's only later a victim might remember how their bully revealed nothing of themselves. Discover something damaging about them and you immediately become an enemy. To a bully, a bully support is temporary and there are others queuing to take that place.

Though bullies offer their supporters reflected glory they remove this on a whim. It is like accepting the benefice of a medieval King; you receive the manor, land, servants and largesse but when you fail to provide weapons, goods, hospitality and support the rewards will be removed. Think of King Henry VIII and Thomas Cromwell, who worked closely until Cromwell became too powerful for Henry's paranoid ego.

Bullies are frequently lonely and fearful, despite how strong they might appear. They know the adulation is false. How many minions visit them in prison? How many join them in social exile? How do they know who is friend and who merely a wannabee? A bully trusts no one and no one trusts them. They test potential friends to destruction, ensuring dominion rather than sharing secrets with someone who might betray them.

A bully can only be recognised through behaviour, never appearance. Phrenology is a discredited science that in the 18th century claimed to identify criminal types from examining the contours of the skull. Bullies come from every walk of life, can be intelligent, appear sociable or religious, be teacher's pet or be highly gifted. Fictional characters Moriarty ('the Napoleon of crime') and Hannibal Lecter are sociopaths. It is estimated 1:10 people have sociopathic traits in real life. Sociopath bullies are masters of concealment; the smiling young sociopath who secretly indulges in cruelty to animals, family, friends or neighbours. School tyrant with his/her tantrums. The cold-faced boss looking at their watch as you enter the building then gets you fired under false pretences.

Who is your bully (or that of the person you support)? A small, seemingly angelic boy surrounded by toadies? The shrewish business woman with sharp suit and helmet-hair? The 'helpful' neighbour who ferrets out information then spreads it as malicious gossip? The sweet old lady who sells poisoned cherries at church stalls? The devout priest who buggers boys in the vestry? A devoted daughter who poisons her mother for the insurance money? The Jekyll & Hyde manager everyone fears?

The Fatal Gene
We are cursed and blessed by technology and science. We no longer hunt unless we choose to do so. We do not have to spend time preparing skins for clothing or strip flesh from bones to eat. We employ professional armed forces to fight wars. There are few hunter-gatherers. Many humans spend their working lives in offices, shops, technological parks and other indoor environments. There is little outlet for aggression even among outdoor workers. Modern man's adrenaline most often gets used in road rage, rushing through a junction before the lights change, skirmishing at sales or Friday-night-domestics.

So how is the volatile product of a million years of breeding absorbed into the trivia of daily life? This remains unresolved. Nature gifted us a dynamic force with a double edge; rushes of adrenaline can result in murder and we all carry this potentially explosive payload. There is no sub-species that comprises everyone with murderous intent. There is little division between those predisposed to kill and those who would during a rage.

Child Abuse to Bully Adult

In the 18th century children were considered incapable of feeling and were often cruelly treated. Hence what horrifies us from history books; children working down mines, cleaning chimneys, clearing fluff from moving machinery in Lancashire cotton mills and even at home living brutally short lives. Victorian parents considered it a duty to beat children to save them from sin. The behaviour of Victorian curate Robert Kilvert towards young females would now be considered child abuse.

Sigmund Freud made a mistake when he surmised that parental abuse as reported by child patients was mere fantasy. Though latter regretting his mistake, generations of abused children suffered because they were not believed. It is known that childhood abuse is likely to lead to disturbed behaviour and a tendency to criminality. Many long term prisoners were appallingly treated as children. Bullied children bully – and so on down the generations, unless there is intervention. We are used to even trusted adults exposed as abusers; clerics, social care workers, celebrities and the military. A community police officer recently told me she believes there is now much less sense of community. People turn a blind eye to injustice, fearing the consequences or simply fearing being ridiculed if they turn out wrong. This attitude leaves the plight of vulnerable people likely to be ignored.

Need for Power & Control

Many bullies have little or no self esteem. That is why they seek sycophants who do their bidding. Perhaps bully parents destroyed their confidence, leaving their child a misfit with a potential life wasted in bitterness, recrimination or criminal activity. In humiliating others, bullies gain dominion to buoy themselves up. The reverse, often in the same family, are siblings victims of a bully sibling or bullied outside the family.

Low Self Esteem

All learning comes at risk of failure. Risk is something bullies do not take. The rare gift of leadership is in their bones but unless someone offers support this talent may never see light. Long prison sentences although destroying some prisoners bring out hidden talents in others. The 'Birdman of Alcatraz', an American imprisoned on the island of the same name became a respected ornithologist despite his (incurable) sociopathic personality disorder. He remained disliked by prisoners and wardens but it is the positive redirection of his energies that is considered a triumph of prison reform.

A bully with low self esteem rather than personality disorder might deliberately damage a piece of work by a fellow pupil or a precious item of clothing. They make family laugh at their sibling-victim through some petty humiliation. In offices their humiliation of a victim provides entertainment for bored staff (who do not understand this is bullying). In the forces they might manoeuvre a victim into a dangerous situation, manipulate officers into punishing a victim or ensure an officer-victim loses face. In relationships they destroy a partner's confidence, turn their children against them or conduct affairs with friends or colleagues of the victim-partner. Cruelty, lies, manipulation, spite are a stock-in-trade.

Envy & Greed

A bully perceives a victim has something they cannot have; nice personality, talent, looks, a longed-for object, academic or sporting achievement or, commonly, a love rival. The bully does not consider how much effort it takes to achieve. They want what their victims have but without making effort. If the bully craves riches it is likely what they really want is love not goods. Because they believe love has been denied them, they turn to bullying or acquiring possessions and money. That is why a bully is never satisfied; they can never have enough of anything.

Revenge & Spite

To a bully a victim represents a barrier. It is a paranoid state. Whether the hurt is real, an incident the victim has innocently perpetrated or imagined, the bully nurses a grudge. They revenge themselves on whoever happens to be there; there does not have to be a reason (*although victims often agonise over this*). If they cannot revenge themselves directly they revenge themselves any way they can. Think urban terrorist. A victim might be deliberately injured; a woman in London was recently pushed under a bus by a passing jogger and commuters have been pushed towards arriving trains. Vengeful bullies wreck relationships, escalate fights, ruin a victim's career or falsely accuse them of wrong doing. A vengeful bully puts a victim in the way of harm.

CROSSOVER ROLES

A bully can become a victim and some perceive them as victims. It is not inevitable however. A bully taken out of power might float, unsure which side to take because they fear consequences. Many a dictator like Mussolini lost their life to a mob comprising former victims. Sometimes bullies become socially engaged, find faith or a skill which transforms them, like the Birdman.

Summary of Bully Characteristics

- often a victim of child abuse
- desire power and control
- insecure and isolated
- does not trust others
- does not form close bonds or social relationships
- do not have equal sexual relationships – dominates
- lack of social intelligence / empathy
- lack skills or talent or desire to learn
- do not risk failure, which prevents them learning new skills
- rely on informers and toadies who are unreliable and untrustworthy
- suspicious, fear betrayal
- put down others to raise their own self esteem
- sociopath bullies are ultra-confident (refer to next section)

* * *

SPACE FOR YOUR NOTES:

17: SOCIOPATHS AND NARCISSISTS

- recognising a sociopath
- recognising a narcissist
- danger to vulnerable or sensitive people

About 1 in 20 people have a personality disorder (PD) but there are many forms of PD, most of whom cause no harm to others. Sociopaths and Narcissists are dangerous to sensitive individuals. They use guile and deceit, often appearing charming until they are blocked, whereupon the charm fades and nasty behaviours appear. You cannot detect personality disorder by looking at someone. The best thing to do is learn their characteristics, recognise and avoid them.

Recognising a Sociopath

Sociopathic personality disorder does not appear in DSMV, the updated American diagnostic manual Western psychiatrists use to diagnose mental illness. However, this is a recognised personality disorder. Sociopaths cannot reform because they are not born with a conscience (ability to be moral) and are blind to morality. There is no cure and they cannot be educated into morality. Sociopaths who commit murder are called psychopaths in the media but this term is no longer used by professionals. It could be argued these individuals are not responsible for 'how they are' as they have an incurable disorder – yet their repulsive acts and behaviours stretch the definition of humanity. Think of the Moors murderers, Myra Hindley and Ian Brady, or Fred and Rose West. Not every sociopath murders but their impulsivity, disregard for others and lack of conscience are likely to lead to criminality.

Intellectual sociopaths and narcissists charm people because of their wit; but these are deceptive traits. These individuals are highly dangerous to sensitive people whom they manipulate and bully mercilessly. Sociopaths are clever and manipulative. They use persistent psychological bullying to get what they want. Individuals without a mentor or supportive family are likely to become serial offenders. Cognitive behavioural therapy is used to help control their behaviour but only works if they agree to enter therapy. Most enter therapy through a court order and are treated in prison. Sociopaths have recognisable character traits:

- rarely reveal information about themselves and readily lie
- seek information about an intended victim
- gain trust then use what they know about a victim to destroy them
- test victims to see if they can be easily manipulated
- accomplished liars and manipulators
- grandiose with strong sense of superiority
- often say things which can be taken two ways, to confuse victims
- psychological cuts to the victim will increase in intensity
- highly obsessional with compulsive behaviour
- cold personality incapable of empathy / remorse
- superficial charm that easily turns to rage
- long time grudge bearers
- take risks to achieve their ends
- highly promiscuous with no feelings for partner

Recognising a Narcissist
Narcissism is a personality disorder defined in DSMIV. Narcissus in Greek mythology was a beautiful youth obsessed by his looks, spending his life gazing at his reflection in a pond. Out of pity, the gods turned Narcissus into the flower that bears the same name. As their name suggests, narcissists are self important, exaggerate, seek attention and are obsessed by their looks. They give little or no attention to others and want

favours that they never return. They make poor partners or spouses. Read Alexander McCall Smith's series 44 Scotland Street; the character Bruce fits the profile of a narcissist. Surprisingly, deep down these individuals often feel inferior with hypersensitivity to slights, despite their lack of empathy to others. Like sociopaths they get in a rage over nothing, never apologise and insult people outrageously. They do not have a sociopath's capacity for cruelty but are difficult to deal with.

Danger to Vulnerable / Sensitive People
If you are a sensitive, kind person you might excuse the behaviour of a sociopath or narcissist, and attempt to reform or change them. Good people have been murdered because they showed their vulnerabilities to a sociopath; that is how dangerous they are. You will never win because they use what they learn about you to destroy you and manipulate others against you. You will find yourself at the butt of outrageous behaviour that gets out of hand as they draw in family, neighbours and friends to support them. If you live next door to such individuals it is best to move out. As a police officer said to me, peace of mind is worth more than injustice or a determination 'not to let them win'. If you stay, it is you who become unstable. Save outrage to fight social injustices that can be won.

* * *

SPACE FOR YOUR NOTES:

18: THE VICTIM-BULLY (CRY BULLY)

- recognising a victim-bully (cry-bully)
- characteristics

Recognising a Victim-Bully (Cry-Bully)

This type of bully appears fragile to those whose shoulders they choose to cry on. Cry bullies are difficult to catch because they mask cruelty like sociopaths (though cry-bullies have a conscience). They choose a sensitive person to reveal too, taking up their time and energy. Cry bullies are damaged and regardless of suffering around them want all the attention yet offer little in return. A form of cry-bully is the marriage-breaker. They weep on a married lover's shoulder begging them not to leave but disappear once the decree absolute is through. Keen observers notice how quickly they recover when there are no spectators. A popular saying, 'under the velvet glove lurks an iron fist' perfectly describes a victim-bully. Their weapons are rumour-mongering, lies, innuendo. A common pattern for a workplace victim-bully is to gather cronies higher in the pecking order, to support them against the victim. If a senior is unwilling to support them, a cry-bully might start an affair with them to get a psychological advantage. They have no compunction about ruining careers to get back at those who expose them. They will fake illness or self harm to get attention (see also Munchausen by Proxy). With no other options they fake or attempt suicide in the spirit of,' they'll be sorry.' They arrange matters so they will be found; loud music from a flat where they have swallowed pills, a 'last' desperate phone call to a friend. They are divas, hysterics, volatile and dangerous. Why do they act like this? Driven by jealousy, envy and need for power. They want sympathy not an equal relationship. Often abused as children or adults they have little self esteem, little capacity for love and rage against they perceive as having a better life.

Characteristics:
- damaged individuals seeking attention & one-sided friendship
- attention seeking, clinging, tearful, prone to moods and weeping
- bully victim by reporting them for imagined hurts
- threaten to kill themselves if victim abandons them, rage like a child's tantrum
- manipulate others against the victim [cf frenemy]
- spiteful / blaming / cannot take criticism
- seek perfect listener / counsellor for themselves in everyone they meet
- seek victims who are kind and naive
- fake illness or faux suicide attempts to get attention

* * *

SPACE FOR YOUR NOTES:

19: THE FRENEMY (FALSE FRIEND)

- recognising a frenemy (false friend)
- characteristics

Recognising a Frenemy (false friend)

The frenemy is a Judas. Whereas a victim-bully wants you as therapist, a frenemy befriends to make trouble. The frenemy is a double agent, fawning over their victim whilst spreading mischief among the victim's friends or widening enmity between rivals. Like spies they live in any country with loyalty to no one. Whatever confidences you share will be turned against you. You might notice how quickly they reveal themselves and ask intimate questions about you. This is the information-gathering stage. They spread gossip and if there is nothing damaging invent it. Protest and you will be given a fake-hurt face as with the cry-bully. Like cry-bullies they are good at fake emotions, targeted double meanings and pretend jokes. They might pressure you and your group to buy something expensive even if they know no one can afford it; an expensive friendship bracelet, trainers or i-pad. They make dangerous or inappropriate dares adding, 'if you don't do [*whatever it is*] I won't be your friend.' A true friend would not say this. When their antics don't work they might turn to cyber bullying (see separate entry), sexting, 'bait out' and malicious rumour-mongering. Give a frenemy free rein and you will cease trusting everyone, leaving former friends wondering what is going on. Their reward is friendship they do not deserve whilst enjoying their power game. Clint Eastwood played such a character in,' Fistful of Dollars'. Think also the Shakespearean portrayal of King Richard III; Bette Davis film, 'Whatever Happened to Baby Jane' and romantic comedy, 'My Best Friend's Wedding' (see Resources/ film). A victim, selected for innocence, will not suspect until a small error rings alarm bells. By then the frenemy will be long gone.

Characteristics:
- approaches a victim seeming anxious to gain friendship
- puts victim off-guard with kindness, gifts and a listening ear
- double agent – seeks and befriend the friend's enemies
- absorb more than they give out
- isolate victim through malicious gossip /tell lies if there is no gossip
- turn to sexting, cyber-bullying or threats when charm fails
- manipulate target and friends to reckless or dangerous acts
- use personal information to humiliate or destroy
- clever at covering up/blaming victim
- react with fury or false tears if found out

* * *

SPACE FOR YOUR NOTES:

20: THE BULLY SUPPORT

- recognising a bully support
- crossovers
- characteristics

Recognising a Bully Support

A bully support eggs bullies on. Some are awaiting a chance at taking on a bully's empire. On a national scale bully supports are potential dictators and empire builders. On the criminal level they are gang members. In the community, they join youths committing ASB. In workplaces they spread malicious rumours. At school they are junior tyrant's cronies. Neither loyal nor honest they will betray a bully without compunction. It is easier to take on a ready-made empire and less risk; which says something of their character. They are less overtly aggressive than the bully, seeking reflected glory. Not possessing charm or aggression, toadies get secondary pleasure watching others suffer. Their overwhelming need is to belong, no matter how much they have to demean themselves.

Crossovers

Aggressive bully supports turn into bullies. They are equally likely to become floaters, waiting to see which side wins. Or they become bystanders but never support a victim.

Characteristics

- no leadership skills to form gang of their own
- too fearful to take bully role
- Likely to be an ex-victim, abused in childhood / as an adult
- isolated – need constant stroking
- the gang becomes family – strong need to belong
- low self esteem

- malicious, sadistic
- betray for reward, no loyalty
- run at first sign of trouble

* * *

SPACE FOR YOUR NOTES:

21: THE FLOATER

- recognising a floater
- characteristics

Recognising a Floater

Floaters wait to see where they will benefit before joining a side. Floaters run if there is trouble, join upstanders if it makes them look good (*as long as there is no risk of being targeted*) or watch passively as bullying continues. Lacking empathy or the will to act, these are shadow-seekers who avoid confrontation and get thrills by watching – like peephole viewers in brothels. Floaters do not become bully supports or upstanders because this involves risk and effort. A floater might have been a victim and fear being bullied again. They cannot break out. With support and over time they might become upstanders but it is equally possible they will use strength to become bullies.

Characteristics

- low self esteem
- need verification of being in a group
- abused as children or victim-adults
- observe before joining winning side
- too fearful to say what they think
- lack confidence – no sense of who they are

* * *

SPACE FOR YOUR NOTES:

22: THE BYSTANDER

- recognising a bystander
- TYPES
- characteristics

Recognising a Bystander

A bystander is someone who sees a victim being bullied but does nothing. They are not bullies themselves. I have identified four types of bystander.

TYPES

The **naive bystander** is in denial. Though they observe bullying, they convince themselves it is not happening or hesitate in case they make a mistake. It is easy for bullies to convince naive bystanders that the victim is a bully. Often a victim does not admit they are being bullied, fearing reprisals, so it is easy to understand why a naive bystander is hesitant to act. This situation is common in families where it is taboo to accept outsider help. It also explains why over-kind social workers can be easily convinced by abusers there is 'no problem' and abused children end up in mortuaries.

The **passive bystander** sees bullying but does nothing. They might tell family or colleagues but would never consider report it, let alone supporting the victim, remonstrating with the bully or bully supports.' It's not my problem' and 'someone else will do something' are bread and butter to a passive bystander. The passive bystander forms the majority of a crowd.

The **fearful bystander** fears reprisal. They worry about themselves, family and friends. Though moved by a victim's plight fear wins through and they step aside from conscience and duty.

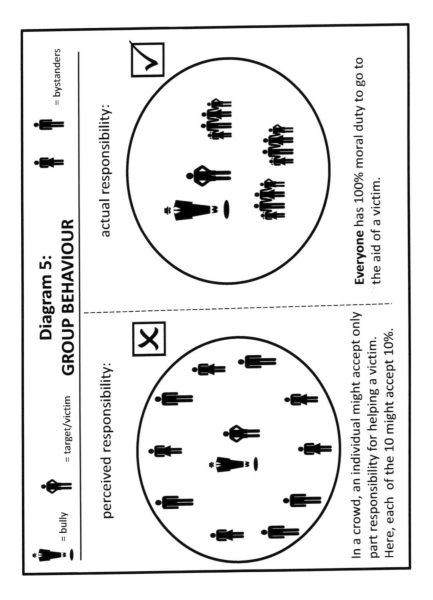

Diagram 5: GROUP BEHAVIOUR

= bully
= target/victim
= bystanders

perceived responsibility:

actual responsibility:

In a crowd, an individual might accept only part responsibility for helping a victim. Here, each of the 10 might accept 10%.

Everyone has 100% moral duty to go to the aid of a victim.

Characteristics
- witness bullying but fail to act
- may be former or current victim
- naive – do not realize bullying is happening; too nice to 'accept' bullying going on or hope it will stop and people will be nice OR fear reprisals or making wrong decision.

* * *

SPACE FOR YOUR NOTES:

23: THE UPSTANDER

- recognising an upstander
- TYPES
- characteristics

'Is he condemned to silence? Let him aid his fellow citizens by silent public witness.' Seneca

Recognising an Upstander

An upstander is someone prepared to confront a bully, comfort a victim or mediate between factions. Upstanders risk alienating the bully, victim and bystander if they get it wrong. They have strength of commitment, not necessarily lacking fear but a strong sense of justice allows them to make themselves heard. It is not a popular position so they must be resilient and prepared for opposition, apathy or both. Many hail from the caring professions. Individuals considered bumptious in other situations become upstanders. They are not phased by public opinion or moral panics but work quietly to resolve often very difficult situations BUT it is as well to remember some upstanders are doing it for personal gain or glory. If a victim denies they are being bullied though bullying is clear to onlookers, an upstander will support the victim, encouraging them to seek help. They are prepared to suggest bullies seek help. These psychologically-sound individuals are likely to have been victims or bullies and are therefore highly motivated to drive change.

TYPES

A **diplomatic upstander** does not pin blame but mediates. They are not afraid to confront despite a degree of personal danger, physical or psychological. These individuals often work behind the scenes.

A **glory-seeking upstander** does what they do for kudos

or reward. Cynically, one might say, prominent people like celebrities, senior managers, politicians and leaders make use of bully situations to be seen 'sorting out a social problem'. This type of upstander are trailed by an 'in crowd'; pressure group, religious organisation, political party or HR department. You detect them from frequent smiley appearances in newspapers and TV reports, shaking hands with victims, families or reformed bullies. In groups you see them during widely-publicised crimes such as the murder of Stephen Lawrence or the Moors-murders, offering opinions on how the law should be changed or 'what went wrong'. Despite the often-dubious reason for their actions, these are nevertheless strong individuals who make a difference.

The **silent or quiet upstander** will, as Seneca suggests, (epigram at head of section) quietly support a victim. You do not need to speak out to be supportive nor is everyone capable of doing so. School anti bully ambassadors can simply stand next to and talk to a victim, showing the bully this person is not isolated.

Characteristics of an Upstander
- stand by a victim to demonstrate support
- may be prepared to confront a bully
- seek out and help victims
- encourage victims and bullies to seek help
- not phased by unpopularity or danger
- contribute to bringing about change
- is likely to have been bullied or be a reformed bully

* * *

SPACE FOR YOUR NOTES:

24: THE ANTI BULLYING AMBASSADOR

- role
- characteristics

Role

Anti bullying ambassador is a new role, part of the Government-lead guidelines for reducing bullying in schools. They are recruited from senior pupils and tasked with supporting victims of bullying in the playground or quiet areas where bullying is likely to take place. They encourage victims by talking to them in the bully's presence to show the victim is not excluded (*isolation is a common 'excuse' for school bullying*), or sitting next to a victim on a 'buddy bench,' a seat where a victim can wait for an anti bullying ambassador to support them.

Characteristics

Anti bullying ambassadors usually volunteer for altruistic reasons. It is good training for working life and encourages development of values. Even where the role is taken for kudos, it enables victims and reinforces the message that bullying will not be tolerated. Strong and resilient, not fearing censure or reprisal, this role is for individuals with a strong sense of identity who are not phased by moral panics or criticism. They hail from families brought up to show respect for others no matter their condition, disability, ability or class. Equally they might have experienced deprivation, been given help and now campaign for justice in their own right. They have to put the role before their own needs and thus demonstrate patience, the ability to delay gratification and understand a wide range of behaviours and cultures. This is excellent training for those wishing to work in the humanities, social work, caring professions or be good parents.

* * *

SPACE FOR YOUR NOTES:

LEVEL 3: HUMAN DYNAMICS

25: DYSFUNCTIONAL ROLES: VICTIM/BULLY/RESCUER /HALO EFFECT

- victim, persecutor, rescuer
- sub sets
- the halo effect
- changing behaviour under duress

Humans relate dynamically. That is, relationships change over many dimensions:

➤ form – enmity, friendship, love, affiliation
➤ emotion – happy, sad, poignant, love struck, anxiety, fear
➤ intensity – weak, strong, variable, stuck, forced
➤ value – close, familiar, distant, raw, fresh
➤ time – long term, short term, sporadic, fleeting

The reasons for these changes are likewise variable:

➤ past negative events colour present events
➤ past positive events colour present events
➤ cultural upbringing
➤ expectation of the relationship
➤ personal flexibility
➤ level of ability to understand other views (empathy)

Those with a broader understanding of dynamics together with wide experience of cultures and environments are more likely to experience happiness through relationships. Also, a greater ability to understand and adapt to those around them. Staff in the caring professions are taught human dynamics, but most people are not aware of their existence let alone know how they work. Particularly valuable is how thoughts, feelings and behaviours link, an element in stress management courses. Humans are flexible but under duress tend to return to old negative habits. That is why you need to keep working on this chapter, using a diary or journal to record progress. It is easy to forget how things were and a diary enables you to look back and learn what worked and what did not.

This chapter covers several models of human behaviour. For those unused to a psychological approach, they can appear confusing but make more sense when you start applying them in your own life. Take one model at a time, applying it a personal situation and record what happens. You might find one model works better and this is fine, but do understand the others too – give yourself a larger toolkit!

Victim, Perpetrator, Rescuer

Victim, perpetrator, rescuer was a theory developed by Stephen Karpman, a student of Eric Berne (*who developed transactional analysis or TA theory*). This theory helps us understand toxic relationships in terms of three roles – victim, perpetrator [or bully] and rescuer. Although the rescuer appears altruistic, Karpman believed the role is based on blaming a weaker party (the bully), offering no insight to allow the cycle to be broken. A rescuer (*in this theory*) is only rescuing to play-act 'good boy/ girl' and for reward, an activity Berne referred to as stroking. A rescuer therefore has vested interest in continuing the cycle. Karpman saw the roles as interchangeable:

Diagram 6:
VICTIM/BULLY/RESCUER

The 'victim/bully/rescuer' triangle was proposed by Stephen Karpman (based on his mentor, Eric Berne's, transactional analysis).

Notice the crossover where circles overlap; this is the Upstander's view – the mediator. A diplomat, the Upstander tries to understand all views.

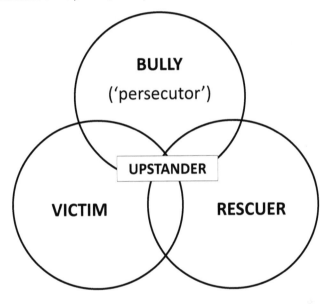

When a rescuer tires of the role they can turn persecutor. A tormented victim turns on a rescuer (who becomes victim). The persecutor becomes a victim of a the harried rescuer, shifting the victim to rescuer or bystander. **Anyone is capable of any role.**

Victim:
- adopts the weak position of 'poor me' to gain sympathy
- enjoys the stroking of the rescuer
- gains security by being bullied i.e. they are used to being dominated
- (also, seek domination in sex life e.g. sado-masochism)
- can become persecutor (taking back power) or rescuer (to punish the bully)

Persecutor:
- enjoys power over victim, a control they do not otherwise have
- if harried by a rescuer turn victim to enjoy sympathy from rescuer
- punishes a rescuer (turning the rescuer into a victim)

Rescuer:
- seek the role for reward (stroking)
- coerced by victim (cry bullies) into playing rescuer
- rescuing allows them to forget their problems
- they tire of rescuing and become persecutor out of anger
- become victim if the persecutor takes the rescue role

'Victim/persecutor/rescuer' occur in many situations; school, work, in families and in the community. In healthy relating, an upstander will not admonish the bully but explain why their behaviour is wrong, helping them move on by discovering and using talents. Similarly, an upstander rescuer encourages victims to find other ways of dealing with a bully, other than being afraid. This might include remonstrating with the bully or walking away (if the bully is a sociopath not open to reason), whilst not losing sight of their achievements and successes. Victims, over time, tend to lose confidence and self esteem. Victim/persecutor/

bully does not allow victims to move on, because both bully and rescuer have a vested interest in maintaining the victim's role. Healthy relating offers better options for maintaining everyone's mental wellbeing and happiness.

Sub Sets

In the diagram, 'Key Players – motives & interactions,' I describe subtypes. For persecutor, note I substitute the word bully and added in the roles of bystander, floater and bully support.

Changing Behaviour Under Duress

It was in our primitive nature to be part of a tribe and this has not altered. The consequences are usually positive but group dynamics alter the way people behave. In bullying, damage is done to a victim when bystanders blame them, after being convinced by a bully the victim is to blame. This perceived victory gives a bully power and leads to the victim becoming more fearful (see diagram 7 overleaf).

Bystanders or observers are changed too; perhaps fearing being drawn in, or thrilled by the power and becoming bully supports or appalled and becoming upstanders. It is easy to understand why duress (stress) can lead to extreme changes in character but those who are psychologically unaware find this difficult to understand.

The Halo Effect

Walk into any room and strange things happen. One or two people will immediately like you. Someone will dislike you. The majority will appear not to take an opinion until they get the measure of you. Yet everyone in that room will look at you and immediately form an opinion. If you remind them of someone they like, they will like you or the other way around. Once this

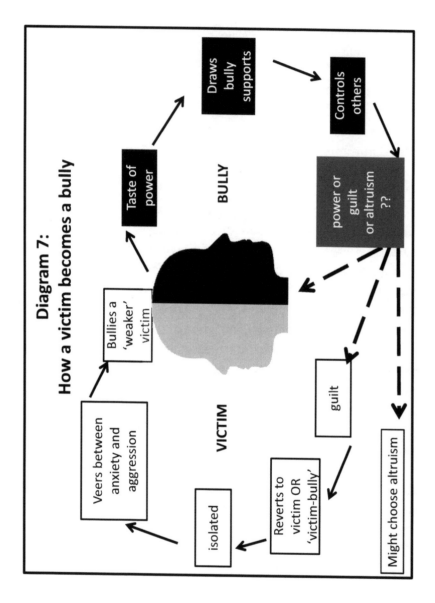

Diagram 7:
How a victim becomes a bully

opinion has been made, it is difficult to shift, no matter how outrageous your behaviour. Ask any murderer's spouse about a partner who has committed murder and they inevitably claim this was 'completely out of character.' This is the halo effect in action.

If we like someone, we assume they are good all through like a stick of rock. Unfortunately everyone has the capacity for wickedness but some resist more easily. In bully situations involving popular pupils, public figures or perceived 'good' managers, it is common for bystanders to rush to their side. The individual not so well known is likely to become scapegoat as everyone points a finger of blame. This can start with one person supporting the bully and spread like a chain reaction, particularly where there are malcontents seeking a cause. This situation is called a toxic environment and its characteristics are well documented. Think about it – this is how totalitarian states operate. The protagonist (causal factor) tries to avoid blame by getting supporters to find evidence against the victim. Look at the examples I gave earlier; 16th century witch hunts and German citizens in World War II being persuaded by Hitler to accept his 'final solution' for Jews.

* * *

SPACE FOR YOUR NOTES:

26: PERCEPTIONS: BLACK, WHITE & GREY THINKING

PERCEPTION & ATTITUDE
black thinking
white thinking
grey thinking

PERCEPTION AND ATTITUDE

Our attitude to any given situation depends on one of three types of thinking (refer to diagram 8 opposite, Perception). These are not fixed behaviours but depend on 'how we see' what happens in the world around us:

➢ black thinking – negative thinking.
➢ white thinking – over-optimistic thinking
➢ grey thinking – realistic; accepting 'what is'

Black and **white thinkers** are inflexible. White thinkers are over optimistic whereas black thinkers believe nothing works and nothing will. Low mood can often trigger the over-hopefulness of white thinking that things will work out – the attitudes of film characters Pollyanna and Poppy (refer to Resources, films). Pollyanna and Poppy are irritating because they refuse to admit anything negative happens in the world. Though we initially like them, over time their sugariness becomes jarring. They are adult-children who refuse to grow up letting others bear their stress. Pollyanna and Poppy types in real life eventually break down, because they have learn to cope with life's difficulties. Let me offer a garden metaphor based on advice from Alan Titchmarsh! Imagine a tree has been tied and staked all the way up the stem to counteract winds. Once the stakes and ties are removed the branches will break off when subjected to strong wind, because they have never become supple through

Diagram 8: Perception
Black, White & Grey Thinking

1. We think about the future 3 times more than we think about the past
2. When certain chemicals are depleted, thinking turns black or white
3. When anxious/in low mood, we filter out positive, hopeful messages
4. We experience every type of thinking – to different degrees

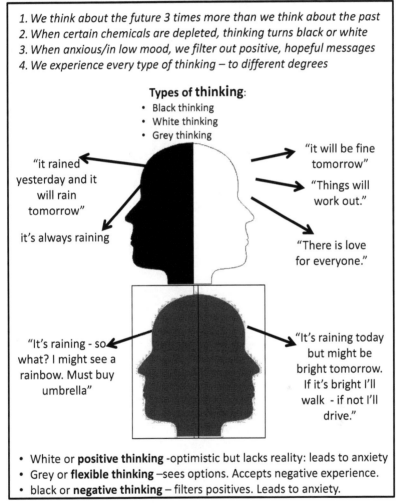

Types of thinking:
- Black thinking
- White thinking
- Grey thinking

"it rained yesterday and it will rain tomorrow"

it's always raining

"it will be fine tomorrow"

"Things will work out."

"There is love for everyone."

"It's raining - so what? I might see a rainbow. Must buy umbrella"

"It's raining today but might be bright tomorrow. If it's bright I'll walk - if not I'll drive."

- White or **positive thinking** -optimistic but lacks reality: leads to anxiety
- Grey or **flexible thinking** –sees options. Accepts negative experience.
- black or **negative thinking** – filters positives. Leads to anxiety.

flexing. The tree's stem grows brittle and therefore weak. But a tree staked low down and allowed to flex grows stronger as it moves with the wind. The Chinese have a saying, 'a reed must bend when the wind blows,' which amounts to the same thing.

Grey thinkers are more realistic, accepting life comprises positive and negative and that it is up to us to find ways of coping. Grey thinkers are adaptable. Though they still experience sadness, disappointment and anxiety they are bolstered by success, good experiences and happy events. Grey thinking accepts what is; that even seemingly never-ending rain will end, given time. Grey thinking finds benefits in the negative, that rain fills water butts and we can do indoor pastimes. For a happy, stable life, we need to aim toward grey thinking.

Over time, we use all three types of thinking but tend to revert to our overt type in times of stress. Black or white thinkers are thrown by situations because their emotions rise and fall with events. How we think affects mood. It is vital to adopt grey thinking as a habit.

* * *

SPACE FOR YOUR NOTES:

27: THE TRIANGLE OF INSIGHT: THINKING, FEELING, BEHAVIOUR

- triangle of insight (refer previous diagram)
- example
- the adaptable human

The Triangle of Insight

The model 'victim/persecutor/rescuer' helps us understand what happens in dysfunctional relationships. The model 'Perceptions: black, white and grey thinking' helps us see how our attitude has a strong bearing on we feel. The 'triangle of insight' (refer to earlier diagram) ties these together. This model helps us understand the relationship between thinking, feeling and behaviour; also how this connects to well- being and happiness.

Our reactions (behaviour) are strongly affected by what happened in the past. This affects how we feel and subsequently how we behave. As a result, we feel distressed or happy and under similar situations we will feel the same – until a later experience causes us to think differently.

> **Example**. 'I see a bully. I remember last time I ran off and cried. As a result I felt depressed. This time, I choose to look the bully in the eye, say hello then walk off. As a result I feel confident. The next time I see the bully, he is confused. He does not know what to expect. He thought I would run away and cry. But seeing him again, I say hello. As the confused bully starts to insult me, I tell him/her they need help then walk off slowly.
>
> I feel happier because things are changing. I do not know what will happen next but am armed knowing I can do something I choose, **not** what the bully expects. He/she

has not forced me to do something I did not want and that gives me more confidence. I know sometimes he/she may 'get under my skin' but I stay calm, knowing I can do something different again..'

The Adaptable Human

From black thinking, the person in this example moves to grey (adaptable) thinking. They need to be aware it is not good to move to white thinking, because they will not be prepared when the unexpected happens. Bullies seek victims who are likely to behave the way they expect, which is not to make a fuss. Do something different and, mostly, they will find another victim. If not, block and 'box clever' so they never know what to expect. The trick is not to be phased by a bully's behaviour but act according to what is right for you. However, if there is physical danger, never confront a bully but walk off.

As a result of practising we become flexible like the tree which, staked near the bottom of the trunk, flexes when the wind blows. When we are flexible we take knock-backs without giving up. We repeat what works or do something different. As Ericksonian Therapists would say, 'change your behaviour and keep the change.' When we flex, our emotions grow positive. Your body language reflects this whether you realize or not. Notice the difference between how a victim moves and how someone with self confidence moves. Watch cartoon Tom and Jerry. Jerry mouse wins because he uses his resources against Tom the cat to outfox his persecutor.

Humans are highly adaptable. Stoics realized this two thousand years ago. We respond positively after success. Unlike animals, man can adapt to infinite environments which is why we survived when other species became extinct. Anxieties will always arise but by constantly taking new approaches we are utilising very effective primitive mechanisms. And by studying our own psychology we gradually gain the upper hand over Neanderthal-like bullies who fail to adapt.

* * *

SPACE FOR YOUR NOTES:

LEVEL 4: AGGRESSION, FEAR AND ANGER

28: BASIC INSTINCTS – A SUMMARY

Fear, anger and aggression along with jealousy lie at the root of most bullying. Yet these seemingly negative emotions are vital to survival (explained later). They cause problems because we live in a different world to our primitive ancestors with few outlets for expressing strong emotion. These emotions were once dispersed in hunting, then later in history in hand-to-hand combat, riding, rioting or watching public hangings. The closest we get to these safety valves are reacting at sports matches, playing energetic sport, having sex, watching races, gang fights and what the police call, 'Friday-night domestics.' Unfortunately, many pent-up frustrations are expressed through bullying.

It is estimated 1 in 2 people experienced bullying which is shocking. So what can we do? First is to understand our nature, the dynamics I covered in the previous section. Understanding goes a great way toward prevention among thinking people. It is better to act than react; this is empowering even if the other party does not follow suit.

Our emotions are hard-wired in our DNA. We know, thanks to Freud, they arise in a complex area he called 'mind.' Some scientists believe mind is located in the brain, others that it is contained in special cells throughout the body. Thanks to Behaviourists like Skinner we know thinking, feeling and behaviour are linked and how changing one changes the other two. We know a great deal about personality, the cluster of emotions and behaviours which make us who we are. Like Lego, a few components arranged in infinite variation allows each of us to be unique. We know emotions are the result of stimuli which trigger chemicals to flood certain organs, preparing body/mind for stress; the 'flight/flight/freeze' which enabled man to survive down generations. What has not completed is a physical adaptation to modern life. Our lives are too short to perceive Darwinian adaptation in action.

* * *

SPACE FOR YOUR NOTES:

29: FIGHT/FLIGHT/FREEZE

Imagine the harsh lives of hominids 200,000 years ago. Hominids lived alongside carnivores which were larger, stronger and faster. For millions of years carnivores had preyed on plant eaters (herbivores) and smaller prey and food was plentiful. As far as carnivores were concerned, when hominids appeared they were another type of prey. But hominids grew to like meat too. Fast adapting apes discovered herbivores were easy to catch and carnivores best avoided. Hominids had to respond quickly:

- fight – chase and kill prey
- flight – run from large carnivores or dangerous enemies
- freeze – play dead if a carnivore was too close to run away

In the diagram, 'fight, flight, freeze', Jumblies represent species which failed to adapt. Though some insects and small animals could successfully 'play dead' as camouflage, this was too risky for larger creatures. Jumblies soon died out. Lions can run fast but rarely need to, being top predators. Man can switch from fleeing to hunting as well as adapting to unfamiliar landscapes. With greater adaptability, hominids quickly spread through the world, becoming dominant species. Their large brain size enabled fast thinking and thus greater survival potential. Fight, flight, freeze is common to all mammals but man's advantage was greater capacity to learn quickly, not only hunting in packs but using clever techniques like cooperative hunting. Fight/flight/freeze prepares the body for action, as soon as a trigger is received by one of our senses. A trigger floods appropriate organs with chemicals, sending power to the muscles and heart to aid fast running. Let's examine two of these vital chemicals, adrenaline and testosterone.

* * *

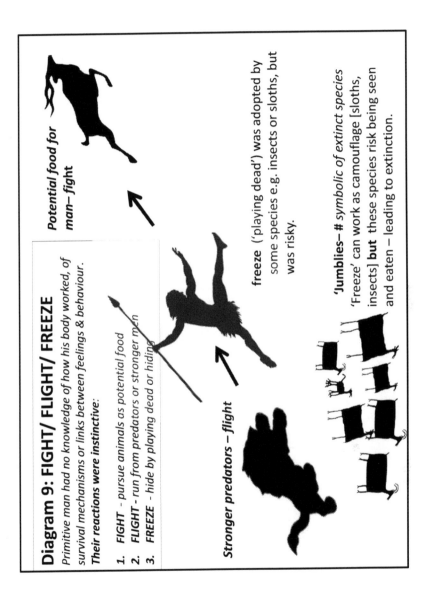

Diagram 9: FIGHT/ FLIGHT/ FREEZE

Primitive man had no knowledge of how his body worked, of survival mechanisms or links between feelings & behaviour.
Their reactions were instinctive:

1. **FIGHT** - pursue animals as potential food
2. **FLIGHT** - run from predators or stronger men
3. **FREEZE** - hide by playing dead or hiding

Potential food for man—fight

Stronger predators – flight

freeze ('playing dead') was adopted by some species e.g. insects or sloths, but was risky.

'Jumblies– # symbolic of extinct species
'Freeze' can work as camouflage [sloths, insects] **but** these species risk being seen and eaten – leading to extinction.

SPACE FOR YOUR NOTES:

30: ADRENALINE AND TESTOSTERONE

- adrenaline
- breathing & fight/flight/freeze

Adrenaline (see diagram)

Adrenaline is stored in the adrenal glands, sited on top of the kidneys. When released adrenaline has marked effects:

1. heart beats fast, sending blood to the muscles resulting in pale, clammy skin, shivering or sweating and high blood pressure.
2. lungs expand, enabling rapid breathing and gulps of air to increase pace
3. digestion slows, leading to churning stomach and dry mouth
4. faeces and urine are ejected to lighten the body for running
5. Pupils dilate to focus, leading to a wide eyed 'tunnel vision' look.
6. muscles contract, causing twitching, fluttering, hair-on-end and shaking legs

Have you noticed something? Consider the effects of fear, anger, aggression, love and re-read the reactions above. Interesting isn't it? People describe shitting in fear which is a natural reaction to stress. Anyone feeling nervous will have an urge to defecate which will lighten the body for action. Whether fearful or angry, our pupils dilate and we breathe fast. People declaring love or feeling anxious describe butterflies in the stomach. These are not arbitrary but primitive reactions; fight/flight/freeze in action. Providing no further stress is encountered, adrenaline dissipates after 20 minutes (refer to diagram, Adrenaline). To deal with excess adrenaline go to level 1, Empowerment where I explain re-breathing.

Breathing and Fight/Flight/Freeze

Primitive man running from a lion or chasing potential prey? What appear panic symptoms are the physical effects of flight/fight/freeze as the body prepares for action. This manifests fast breathing which can seem like a heart attack with palpitations, dilated pupils, tingling sensations, chest constriction (refer to diagram, Adrenaline). The symptoms will always manifest the same for the same person. If you are worried about heart attack it is advisable to get symptoms checked at A&E, but be reassured that over 90% of people attending for suspected heart attack turn out to be natural reactions to adrenaline flooding. What actors/sportsmen describe as performance nerves amount to the same thing (see diagram 10 opposite):

1. hormones flood the body, readying it for action
2. results in tremors, palpitations, butterflies, dilated pupils, headache, defecating / urinating, sweaty palms and under-arms.
3. you react without thinking (to get out of danger)

Ruminating can lead to panic about what will happen. This leads to avoidance and then phobia. Luckily, primitive man did not ruminate. Panic did not prevent him going hunting next day or we would not be here; me writing this and you reading it. Our body has only one alert system. Perhaps it confuses us by its simplicity. Autonomic systems work outside awareness; for example, we do not need to think about breathing.

Normal breathing takes in oxygen, distributing it to the brain and muscles where it refreshes the blood. In fight/flight a large amount of oxygen is ingested through fast, shallow breathing which enables fast running. The used oxygen is breathed out as carbon dioxide. During panic attacks, symptoms repeat because there is no action to use the oxygen, so you keep experiencing

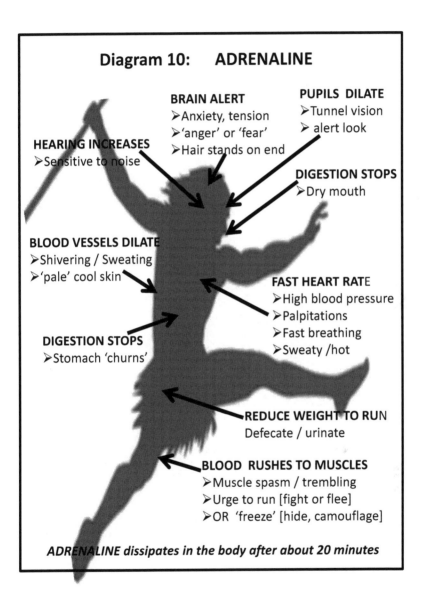

Diagram 10: ADRENALINE

BRAIN ALERT
➤Anxiety, tension
➤'anger' or 'fear'
➤Hair stands on end

PUPILS DILATE
➤Tunnel vision
➤ alert look

HEARING INCREASES
➤Sensitive to noise

DIGESTION STOPS
➤Dry mouth

BLOOD VESSELS DILATE
➤Shivering / Sweating
➤'pale' cool skin

FAST HEART RATE
➤High blood pressure
➤Palpitations
➤Fast breathing
➤Sweaty /hot

DIGESTION STOPS
➤Stomach 'churns'

REDUCE WEIGHT TO RUN
Defecate / urinate

BLOOD RUSHES TO MUSCLES
➤Muscle spasm / trembling
➤Urge to run [fight or flee]
➤OR 'freeze' [hide, camouflage]

ADRENALINE dissipates in the body after about 20 minutes

symptoms then wrongly attribute them to anxiety. Slow deep breathing (or re-breathing using a paper bag) reduces oxygen and calms the mind. Never use a plastic bag unless you want to end up in a mortuary!

* * *

SPACE FOR YOUR NOTES:

31: HOW INSTINCTS CONNECT WITH BULLYING

1 Million Years BC (the film)

The film, '1 million Years BC' depicts very well the development of emotional responses. Despite historical inaccuracy i.e. dinosaurs and man interacting (*dinosaurs were extinct 64 million years before hominids arrived*), this film is fetching, with its fur bikinis and man-shorts, and educational. The story depicts interaction between two tribes, the Shell and the Rock. Raquel Welch plays Luana of the social, artistic Shell Tribe. John Richardson plays Tumak of the aggressive, warring Rock Tribe. The Shell Tribe develop altruism, community, art and romance whereas the Rock Tribe remain aggressive. When Tumak is expelled from his tribe he joins the Shells, saves Luana from several encounters with dinosaurs and is welcomed into their tribe. At the end of the film there is a volcanic eruption which kills many of both tribes. The Shell Tribe move to find a new home, inviting survivors of the Rock Tribe to join them.

Even in this saga you see problems brewing. What will happen when the surviving Rock people begin life among the peace-loving Shells? Some individuals have a greater propensity to aggression, then as now, and it is likely leadership fights will break out. How will they cope with this? Though the primitive intellect was as developed as ours, primitives were not aware of their psychology (cause and effect). It took thousands of years before Freud enabled us to understand our psychology. What enabled primitives to survive causes modern man problems. Most of us do not live in the bush, hunt or run from lions. Getting a mate no longer requires large surges of testosterone. We don't have to forage food. So where does excess energy get used? How do emotions get resolved? Primitive mechanisms took millions of years to develop but modern living has advanced so rapidly evolution has not caught up:

➢ We have the same reactions to fight flight freeze as primitive man
➢ few people are aware of their psychology
➢ many are unable to cope with emotions / social situations
➢ some have short triggers
➢ some have excessive amounts of testosterone
➢ this can turn into fighting, self-harm, suicide & bullying

On the reverse side, Freud and his followers the Behaviourists have shown us how to understand our nature and turn knowledge to advantage.

* * *

SPACE FOR YOUR NOTES:

32: HISTORIC OUTLETS FOR AGGRESSION

From ancient civilisations, through the Dark and Middle Ages, the Enlightenment, the new sciences of the eighteenth century, the cruelties of Victorian times; these were difficult times for ordinary people with danger, disease and dirt. Yet it was these difficulties which used excess stress hormones that today cause many social problems. Verbal abuse has always been used in warfare for intimidation. After a rousing call to arms by the King, warriors took up a battle cry, hate-screaming as they ran at their enemies. Archaeologists have found artefacts depicting Viking Berserker warriors biting shields and foaming at the mouth as they worked themselves into battle readiness. Scotsmen used to raise their kilts to show bare arses in contempt of their enemies. Maori tribesmen performed a Hakka or war dance, making grotesque faces, waving their arms, and sticking out their tongues(*the Hakka is still used by the South African All Blacks team as a pre-match rite*). Second World War soldiers uttered hate-screams as they charged dummy enemies in bayonet practice. Boxers stare or insult each other as a form of intimidation. Why did they do these strange things?

A warrior could not fight in calm mood and nor could a modern-day boxer. They have to work themselves up to produce the adrenaline that gives them an edge. Early warfare was very bloody before cannons and bombs allowed fighting at a less graphic distance. Recent discoveries of Roman and Medieval battleground burials show remains with terrible injuries; not tens but thousands of blood-soaked bodies over which living warriors stepped, sliding through blood, mud and excrement. Battles continued for days or weeks until the leader was killed, surrendered or soldiers deserted. Without aggression, solders would be unable to face such horrors.

For hundreds of years, animal based sport was common entertainment. Medieval fairs had chained bears attacked by dogs; sixteenth century noblemen went stag-hunting on horseback; eighteenth century peasants enjoyed dog and rat fights or chickens with spurs fighting to the death; nineteenth century cat-throwing was popular as were badger baiting, fox hunting and hare coursing. People enjoyed bloody spectacles and betting on the result. In the midst of dirt and drudging, high crime rates with no policing and short disease-ridden lives, seeing animals suffer relieved their own suffering, in the same way as Roman citizens enjoyed gladiatorial spectacles before going back to their humdrum life. Public hangings also served as stress relief. Thousands of visitors picnicked, were entertained by musicians or watched excitedly as they waited for the cart containing the condemned. Those who flaunted death, bowing and making wit with the crowd, were egged through their ordeal with laughter and applause, flowers, food and wine, as they made their way to the drop. This cruel spectator sport was enjoyed across classes. Samuel Pepys and Dr Samuel Johnson were among diarists who attended from curiosity, not stinting the grisly detail. From young to old, hangings were regular holiday treats. Most of these sports are outlawed in our sensitive and mostly moral society. Yet we still have the same amount of adrenaline as our blood-thirsty forbears. And that causes problems in modern societies. Interestingly, this is the same reason bullies enjoy seeing victims suffer. In their view it is morally acceptable to hive negative feelings onto another, especially when others laugh, scream, jeer or applaud. It gives the bully a false sense of power, control and strength. It also gets rid of excess adrenaline and testosterone, for both sexes.

* * *

SPACE FOR YOUR NOTES:

33: PRIMITIVE INSTINCTS IN MODERN MAN

- anger & aggression
- controlling anger

Though living in towns and cities brought freedom from the dangers of solitary life it created problems. History has gone too quickly; man has not had time to adapt to living shoulder-to-shoulder in large numbers. As well as the better traits of civilisation, this also results in resentment, anger, suspicion, greed and desire for power. For things to improve requires leadership; people willing to challenge, be outspoken, fight for peace. There has to be a place for drive and ambition which arise from primitive emotions like anger, envy and fear. These aspects are all potential agents of change.

Anger and Aggression

Many understand bullying as physical or aggressive behaviour. True, bullying can manifest like this but there are other forms. There is an urban myth that nice people do not get angry, as if there is a separate race of violent people. Though many deny they get angry this emotion is a potential in all of us. Aggression lies at the extreme end of anger; anger out of control. Both are emotional reactions to a trigger, just like a cave man sighting a lion, enemy or deer. Alertness triggers adrenalin which turns into anger or aggression when out of control.

Controlling Anger

Though anger might seem a gloomy inevitability, there is hope built in. A time gap. Anger can be calmed in the gap before adrenaline floods the system. Once it floods it overcomes reason. That is why police forces and paramedics are taught to calm down situations, allowing time for adrenaline to diffuse.

- a javelin thrower knows the effect of adrenalin on his/her system and uses the gap between stimulus and action to improve timing; use breathing techniques to send more oxygen to the muscles and steady the nerves ready to choose the best moment to let fly. Breathing deeply, rising on tiptoe, concentrating on the goal, waiting the right moment to run then throw.
- a boxer dances around their opponent waiting for the moment to throw a punch.
- an employee pauses, practising words silently before taking a breath and asking for a raise.
- someone in love takes a deep breath and despite feeling jangling nerves and butterfly stomach, reveal their feelings.
- Anger management courses enable people to use the gap to change their behaviour and thus the connected emotions.

* * *

SPACE FOR YOUR NOTES:

34: ASCENT OR DESCENT FOR MAN?

In future generations will we need 'fight/flight/freeze'? The current answer is YES. Imagine crossing a road and a lorry hurtles toward you. Without adrenaline, you are blasé and walk out.. Instinct saves us from accident, muggers, fire, flood – and bullies. We will always need instinct. However..

Recent research points to reducing levels of testosterone in males and females which scientists believe has been decreasing steadily over time, resulting in changes to skull shape. Researchers measured fossil skulls world-wide, comparing facial changes and from this research it has been concluded hominids are adapting rapidly. Of course, our lives are too short to perceive such changes. Researchers have also looked at the development of burials, art, religious symbolism, human cooperation, altruism, self ornamentation. These mark us out from chimpanzees who are aggressive, territorial and subject to frequent fights. Bonobos, our closest ape relatives, are highly socialised and resolve problems by having sex. Bonobos are postulated to have lower levels of testosterone. Individual identity and behavioural modernity are thought to have begun around 50,000 to 40,000 years ago. Researchers put this civilising effect down to testosterone levels reducing within our species. Even Homo sapiens were more androgyne, less aggressive and dominant than Neanderthals, though recent discoveries show the latter had more artistic leanings than we thought.

Science fiction points to a lessening of sexual differences toward an androgyne figure. There is only one chromosome difference after all. But unless man becomes automaton we will always need a means of getting away from danger which is what testosterone and adrenaline do for us. Read the chapter, 'The Blue Globes', from Ray Bradbury's The Martian Chronicles, which describes interesting possibilities. We live sedentary lives in close proximity. We get angry, suspicious, fearful and embroiled in situations; reacting rather than considering. We prize our moral compass, live relatively care-free lives, have individuality, more than the basics and can assert our rights. Wanting more and more is part of the problem.

Natural selection continues, though it is as difficult to imagine as it is to take in the vastness of the Universe or how fast our planet is hurtling through space. Such things are now the speculation of theoretical physics, cosmology and science fiction. It is speculated that one day in trillions and trillions of years the energy in our Sun will fizzle out and the Universe come to an end. Perhaps that possibility is nearer than we think. But we do our best to become masters of our destiny, masters of our lives. And that begins by learning to live harmoniously and understanding ourselves. In The Time Machine, Victorian writer H G Wells imagined the development of man into two races, Eloi and Morlocks. The Eloi are peaceful, live simple lives but fear night. The time traveller discovers the Eloi are bred for food by the dominant Morlocks, who live underground coming to the surface to collect victims. The Eloi whilst having human awareness do not fight back until the time traveller shows them how. It is a chilling dystopia but it makes you think, about what it is to be human.

* * *

SPACE FOR YOUR NOTES:

LEVEL 5: BULLIES THROUGH HISTORY

35: HISTORIC MEANING OF BULLY AND TARGET (VICTIM)

- the new morality: acceptable aggression v bullying
- victim or target

Historic Meaning of Bully

The word bully has greatly changed meaning over time. In the 15th and 16th centuries, a bully was a sweetheart (girlfriend), a term of endearment describing someone worthy or admirable. By the 18th century the meaning had become sinister, describing blades or gallants fond of fighting, the type preferred by women who admired thugs. In the early nineteenth century a bully dinner was something tasty. This meaning was used ironically by British soldiers in the first world war to describe tinned beef that formed part of their rations. Around the same time, the phrase 'bully for you' expressed delight at good fortune. Over time bully took on the negative meaning it has today to describe someone who deliberately hurts, frightens or torments. The verb to bully means threatening or persecutory acts (Chambers Concise Dictionary). Definitions of bully in my Roget's of 2000 are entirely negative, with synonyms like tyrant, frighten, insolent and malevolent.

The New Morality: Acceptable Aggression v Bullying

Since the advent of popular psychology, bullying is now widely recognised as psychologically damaging and is unacceptable.

Unfortunately, overuse of the word has lead in some cases to overuse, for example used to describe the sort of rough and tumble among boys and young animals that is a normal part of growing up. Therapists are concerned lest overuse of the word bullying will in time diminish empathy for victims or the despair felt by relatives of a bullycide (suicide as a result of bullying).

Concurrently, this new social morality is leading to ostracism of individuals who follow certain career paths. Militia were traditionally lauded by the public; victorious Roman armies paraded in Triumphs as Roman citizens turned out to cheer and throw flowers. Modern soldiers are more likely to face anti-war or human rights demonstration, accusations of atrocity or at best indifference. Seemingly, we have not reconciled human rights with upholding those who carry out our dirty work. Public figures are accused of bully behaviour as some go over the ill-defined line between what is morally acceptable and what is not. Remember the farmer terrified of intruders who spent years in prison for killing a young burglar? There have been countless cases of women murdering a spouse after years of abuse. Guantanamo Bay prisoners complained of guards flouting the Geneva Convention while they were responsible for terrible atrocities on civilians. The Australian penal colonies at Van Dieman's Land (Tasmania) and Norfolk Island were notorious for sadistic guards who flogged prisoners mercilessly and had them in chains for years, with no redress. School bullies like Charles Dickens' fictional Flashman (in 'Tom Brown's Schooldays') have always been despised, yet their characteristics contain the seeds of leadership. 'We cannot prevent bullying', a mental health senior said to me not long since. No, but with insight negative tendencies can be trained to the good. Similarly, victims cannot campaign unless they become assertive.

We need to understand bullying in different environments as

well as its dynamics. Surprisingly there is widespread ignorance about the dynamics of bullying even among HR's. I believe this is why workplace bullying complaints are so often brushed aside and why bullying rarely makes headlines, apart from bullycides.

Target (Victim)

Target is a late Medieval word for a small shield or buckler which was attached to the arm by straps. Later it meant the large targets fixed to the ground that are still used in the same form for longbow and crossbow practice. This was the root of the symbolic meaning of a target (of bullying); the passive receiver of psychological arrows. From the 18th century target took on its present meaning; someone subjected to ridicule.

A victim was originally an animal or human intended for sacrifice (15th century onward). The word victim is now more often used than target in describing an individual at the butt of bully behaviour, especially crime, but I use both in this book. Both are tarnished by a common myth, that victims are weak or passive.

* * *

SPACE FOR YOUR NOTES:

36: THE NATURE OF BULLYING

- what bullying is not
- examples of bullying
- defining bullying
- examples of public bullying

What Bullying Is Not

An occasional shove, even if meant, is not bullying but repeated attacks are. I remember an incident I witnessed in a supermarket years ago when a small boy hit another without provocation. The boys eyed each other before the hitter struck again. Not having children, I was unsure what to do but with insight I wish I had reported this to the responsible adult who was a couple of bays away. My hesitance marks the dilemma of bystanders. I could not assume the second boy (target) had not been goading the first and what I saw was retaliation. Boys fight as part of growing up and learning how to defend themselves. It would have been different if one or the other had drawn blood. What we do is judge situations based on personal experience, which does not necessarily match the situation. But the situation I describe is not bullying. If it had persisted, it would have become bullying. Impassioned debate at University or Parliament is not bullying unless it gets personal. Filibustering is not bullying though it denies free speech by the member waiting patiently to speak. Joking or teasing is not bullying but there are waspish opinions on this. An occasional, exuberant insult in public is let go unless it crosses the line of legislated-against discrimination e.g. insults about race, sexual orientation, faith or disability. A few years ago a man was fined for playing the record, 'Kung Foo Fighting,' as a Chinese family walked past. He claimed he had not seen them but the Judge thought otherwise. There are many unfortunate examples of synchronicity and to legislate for all would send everyone into paranoia. So too a one-off hot-headed insult is not bullying. I am sure most of us have been guilty of that. Finally, the behaviour of militia in war situations is not bullying apart from situations I described earlier. So if the above are not bullying, what is?

Examples of Bullying

If an individual or group chase, hit or abuse an individual, that is bully behaviour. Repeated taunting with the intent of humiliation is also bullying. Remember the schoolteacher who smiled every time you entered class and you just knew, as did everyone else, that before the end of the lesson you would feel two inches tall? That was bullying – though at the time teachers got away with this sort of behaviour. Many have hang-ups about appearance or behaviours that can be traced back to the 1950's when teacher 'jokes' about fitness, weight or appearance were normal.

Domestic violence of any kind, physical or psychological, is bullying as is sexual shaming and cyber bullying. If this behaviour is perpetrated against individuals protected by the Disability Act (race, religion, disability, faith and sexual orientation) it is a criminal offence. Publishing or spreading malicious gossip without foundation is bullying and an offence under civil law (defamation or slander).

Defining Bullying

Bullying is any behaviour intended to humiliate the target, over a period of time. It can be physical, verbal or psychological, face to face or postings on the Internet. It takes different forms in different environments but follows the same definition.

Examples of Public Bullying

Some bullies (e.g. sociopaths) do not care whom they bully; others are capable of making seemingly opposing moral decisions, genuinely believing they are showing care for one individual by bullying others. A case in point is the odd phenomena of public castigation of Camilla in support of Princess Diana. And more recently, Alfie's Army', a spontaneous and quite aggressive demonstration outside Great Ormond Street Hospital in support of a dying child refused what was considered futile treatment by the NHS. Though this group portrayed themselves as fighters for justice on behalf of the child they actually gang-bullied hospital staff, who became terrified of leaving the building. This put the child's parents in an embarrassing situation and they were forced to plead with this group to stop. These are classic examples of good intent turned into bullying, though not by intent. Investigative journalists can also bully by going too far. Bugging rooms in private houses, setting up hidden cameras and using disguised reporters for entrapment, notably 'fake Sheik' Mahzher Mahmoud on behalf of the now defunct, News of the World newspaper. Though Mahmood had won awards for investigative journalism he was eventually convicted of entrapment. Entrapment is dirty journalism; not exposing wrongdoing but seeking sensationalism and/or personal gain. Similarly a BBC journalist and his team pointed cameras into Cliff Richards' home before he had been charged with a crime (and never was).

It is possible for a bully to think they care, whilst carrying out reprehensible behaviour. It is possible to bully through a false belief of defending a vulnerable person – a classic rescuer situation. And it is possible for demonstrators with good intent to become gang bullies.

* * *

SPACE FOR YOUR NOTES:

37: BULLY BEHAVIOUR CLASSED AS CRIME

- damage to property (burglary, arson)
- domestic violence (grievous/ actual bodily harm)
- other physical violence (affray, murder, manslaughter)
- vigilantism (affray, murder, manslaughter)
- scapegoating (hate crime)
- racism (hate crime)
- malicious gossip (libel)
- psychological abuse (threatening behaviour)

Maybe you do not consider crime a form of bullying but it is. The crimes described below hurt, offend and humiliate, are carried out over time and with intent. That is our definition of bullying (refer to section 36)

Damage to Property (burglary, arson)
A bully might deliberately break or damage property belonging to their victim or enter their house to move, mark/damage or frighten the victim. Clothing, sports wear, school work, photographs, gifts and other treasured items are commonly targeted. This might follow threats of violence to the victim, their family and friends. It is what psychologists call deflected action. The bully wants to hurt their victim yet fears legal or social consequences. They know psychological hurt outlasts physical hurt and sadistically enjoy a victim's reaction.

Domestic violence (grievous/actual bodily harm)
Domestic abuse often goes unreported through fear of social backlash. If one partner is in a prominent position or a network where such behaviour would outrage, it is easy to understand why the victim might not want police involvement. So too if children are involved, because of the risk of the children

being taken into care. The power of social workers is as underestimated as their ability to perceive manipulative parents is overestimated. A battered spouse or abuser can love their child/children but lack the social and emotional skills to deal with setbacks. These individuals were often victims of domestic abuse, neglect or sexual abuse, either in a children's home or a household trying to cope with debt, unemployment, disability and/or alcohol/drug abuse. Domestic abuse takes place across classes and income bands. Historically, domestic violence was seen as family business and no concern of the state. In the 18th century wife beating was acceptable even wife selling if a husband wished. Read, 'The Mayor of Casterbridge' by Thomas Hardy. Domestic abuse is now a criminal offence.

Other Physical violence (actual / grievous bodily harm)
There is a long line between rough-and-tumble (no intent of harm) to criminal acts of violence (deliberate intent). When passions are roused through argument or division (differences), physical violence can follow when adrenaline is roused. Physical violence used to be commonplace in the classroom with teachers caning, beating, throwing heavy chalk rubbers, twisting ears or pulling hair. Thankfully, these are in the past, along with whipping of children by Victorian parents. Unable to chastise naughty children, parents might be at a loss at how to control a wayward child. Today's beaten children can become tomorrow's bullies and victims unless the cycle is broken.

Vigilantism (affray, murder, manslaughter)
Vigilantism is not new. Think of 16th century witch hunts; innocent women and men blamed for illnesses, crop failure or the death of livestock, before being tortured by witch hunters and sentenced to hang or burn at the stake. This pattern

continues to this day; individuals incensed by a moral panic and set themselves up as judge and jury. Social housing tenants of Brislington, Bristol, caused the death of Bijan Ibrahim by falsely declaring him a paedophile and demonstrating outside his home, resulting in two thugs beating Bijan to death before setting him on fire. Another case is 'Oliver's Army' which I described earlier. Though vigilante groups believe they hold a high moral ground, their 'blame' of a random person or group makes them bullies. It is frightening to be on the end of targeting because people lose control of reason when incensed, as their adrenaline production increases.

Cyber Bullying (defamation, libel)

Cyber bullying is relatively new, compared to the age of the Internet. This comprises posting cruel, untruthful comment, explicit photographs (without consent), sexual shaming or revealing intimate secrets – again without consent. The object is to shame or humiliate the target and separate them from their group/organisation.

Scapegoating (victimisation) (hate crime)

Scapegoating is when an individual or group is blamed unfairly for all the wrongs in their group or organisation. The individual is thus shamed and a legitimate target for attack even by those outside the clique. This happens frequently in toxic organisations. It is easy to understand how this works by comparing it with the vile treatment of Jews during the Second World War.

First, Hitler blamed Jews for the poverty rampant in Germany. He pointed out the wealth of the Jews who were by traditional money lenders and bankers, rebranding them as greedy usurers who were robbing Germany of wealth and heritage. Next, Hitler used the false science of eugenics to unfavourably compare racial differences between Jews and Aryans (the German race). Having got the German people on his side he offered a 'solution' to the problem he had created. First, he separated Jews by targeting their businesses for attack, issuing curfews and fines, publicly humiliating them then forcing them into ghettoes. Once civilians saw their leader 'winning' against 'dark' forces they colluded with stage two; confiscation of Jews' possessions and homes, before sending them to concentration camps in closed cattle trains. No one asked questions or if they did, they faced a similar fate – mass shootings or the gas chambers. Learning from history, this is the process by which a bully gets rid of a perceived enemy (victim, target);

1. a problem exists which results in in-fighting
2. *[if a problem does not exist, the perpetrator invents one]*
3. the perpetrator points out a target as the root of the trouble
4. outsiders, eager to relieve their stress, perceive the perpetrator a hero
5. the perpetrator now has tacit permission to do what they like to the target, because the group perceive this to be the 'solution' to the problem
6. malcontents within the group, seeing the target humiliated, join the attack
7. everyone thinks the problem resolved
8. if the target dies or disappears, the process begins at 3.
9. if the perpetrator becomes vulnerable, they become target
10. and so on.

Racism (hate crime)
Hate crime is victimisation because of race, sexual orientation, gender, religious belief, appearance, physical or mental disability.

Individuals with low intellect and low emotional intelligence are likely to use differences as an excuse to attack, excusing their behaviour with self-righteous statements – for example, as in the plethora of false jihad. An example of this crime, which is a form of vigilantism, is the horrific murder of disabled Iranian refugee Bijan Ebrahimi, harassed for seven years by neighbours in Brislington before being murdered in 2013. Bijan was murdered when vigilante neighbours wrongly accused him of being a paedophile on a troubled housing estate. Police who dealt with the case were accused of institutionalized racism with several sacked years after Bijan died. Hate crime takes many forms; damage to property, verbal abuse, rumour-mongering, vigilantism, hate mail, physical or psychological attack. It is a criminal offence in its own right.

Malicious Gossip (libel)
Highly understated or misperceived as amusing, malicious gossip is a form of bullying. Once the arena of village gossips, this behaviour is perpetrated across all ages and both sexes. As O'Malley states in, 'Bully Proof Kids', malicious gossip can be 'very entertaining' and that is why it draws people in. What bullies want is attention, not only from bully supports but as large a crowd as possible. Gossip fills a gap for the idle, lonely and marginalised, taking attention from their difficulties as well as a career for psychologically under-developed individuals. Though not a crime per se unless libel is proven, the danger lies in its spread, leading to hate crime, cyber-bullying and vigilantism. Rapid spread is enabled through social media and the fact malicious gossip is not widely perceived as bullying and can be perpetrated by naive innocents drawn in by those with malicious intent.

Psychological Abuse (threatening behaviour)

Psychological abuse is repeated behaviour resulting in the target losing esteem, confidence or experiencing fear. It can be as simple as meaningful looks from a parent holding a strap. The parent does not have to wield the strap; the threat is enough. This is similar to water torture by Japanese guards on prisoners of war. Another example is the behind-the-hand-whispering of two individuals as a target hoves into view, a favourite modus operandi among certain social tenants by way of sport. A good example is from dystopian novel, '1984' by George Orwell (*which coincidentally deals with fake news spread by a totalitarian state*). Enemies of the state about to be tortured know they will be confronted with their worst fear in room 101. This knowledge in itself is enough to make most confess. Psychological abuse can be more long-lasting than physical abuse, spoiling the victim's potential for love, peace, security and happiness.

* * *

SPACE FOR YOUR NOTES:

38: PUGILISM TO PSYCHOLOGY: THE NEW SOCIETY

- pugilistic-minded society
- psychologically-minded society
- moral panic
- moral panic and its impact on public perspective of bullying
- hope for the future

Pugilistic-Minded Society

In pre-history leadership was vital for survival. It was imperative for a tribe leader to be strong, quick witted, handy with fists and weapons, not only hunting potential prey but warding off rivals. Flash forward in history to the age of King Richard III, the last monarch to take part in hand-to-hand battle. Leaders were expected not only to lead an army but to fight. Before altruism and cooperation in society, you had to use your fists or risk being killed by robbers, highwaymen, footpads, revolutionaries or thieves. This acceptance of pugilism followed down the centuries to Victorian times, when men were expected to physically chastise children and wives. It is the rise of psychology and morality that changed this.

Psychology-Minded Society

The change came when Freud, Jung and their followers began to unravel the mysteries of mind. Slowly, human psychology seeped into public awareness. People realized that how you behave has an effect on feelings, which in turn affects behaviour. They knew criminality was not degeneracy (as Benedict Morel believed – see glossary) but partly genetic and part due to negative environmental influences. Whilst not tolerating horrific crime like the 1960's Moors murders, the public began to show tolerance toward less serious offending. There emerged zero tolerance toward abuse of children and attacks on spouses of either sex, also tolerance of differences and disability.

Though it might not often appear this way, the 20th and 21st centuries brought a kinder, tolerant society.

Moral Panic

As well as individual behaviour in bully situations it is vital to understand how moral panics work. A moral panic is where many individuals protest against a perceived injustice or at those who do not adhere to prevailing rules of society. Moral panics can begin out of fear or a sense of injustice. Moral panics are not new; neither were they always to the good.

In the 16th century there was a moral panic about devil worship that went on over 100 years and lead to thousands of innocents being tortured and burned as witches. Protests about poverty among peasants lead to the Peasant's Revolt during which civilian rioters were killed by soldiers. During the 18th century, fear of revolution lead to innocents being chased, their property burned and the unfortunates murdered by the mob. When trades unionism was in its infancy, many protest marches lead to rioting, imprisonment, hangings and murder of civilians. During both World Wars pacifism was decried and those who advocated it dubbed cowards. Women handed out white feathers to civilian men they thought should be fighting, without considering the circumstances or morality of their assumptions. In the early 20th century there was a huge moral panic about single mothers, particularly among the Catholics. The Catholic Church set up institutions where single mothers were incarcerated with their new born babies forcibly removed then put up for adoption without the mother's consent. Some infants were sent to Australia never to see their mothers again. In, 'The Loss Child of Philomena Lee' (the film version is called, 'Philomena') Martin Sixsmith tells the story of an Irish woman's heartbreaking life-long search for her lost child.

However moral panic can result in beneficial change. The 1960's TV drama, Cathy Come Home by Jeremy Sandford (directed by Ken Loach) told a harrowing story of social injustice and homelessness. Actress Carol White portrayed a young mother who became homeless through a series of bad luck and had her children forcibly removed by social workers. This lead to a storm of outrage against homelessness and the charity Crisis was set up with the fledgling charity, Shelter, also receiving widespread support.

Moral Panic and Its Impact on Public Perspective of Bullying

These powerful expressions of public opinion have a strong bearing on how bullying is viewed. Post war the world has (generally) become more psychologically minded, promoting caring communities with widespread protests about injustice. This would have delighted Chartists and early Trades Unionists who had the right idea but went about getting change through violence. On a wave of liberal thinking, anti-bullying campaigns are now popular. Whereas your grandfather or father (depending on your age!) would promote strap and slipper, today's liberal-minded show revulsion toward any type of violence. Mindful of the danger of gun-toting, knife wielding, bomb-making and nuclear weapons, there is widespread commitment toward peace. After the cowardly murder of Stephen Lawrence, right-thinking people view racism and knife-crime with horror. In America, the murder of large numbers of school children by gun-toting peers has lead to students protests for change in the gun law. The last bastions of Flashman-like bullying and corporal punishment by teachers in public schools is long gone. There is huge outrage at the uncovering of historic sexual abuse of children in institutions. The BBC, who could once do no wrong in the eyes of the public, has been castigated for withholding information in the case of paedophile Jimmy Savile – once a public darling.

Hope for the Future

The recent three part BBC documentary on the cowardly, racist murder of Stephen Lawrence reflects changing times. For 25 years Baroness Lawrence worked tirelessly for justice, uncovering corruption and failures which shocked the public. The Lawrence's devotion to justice promulgates the society we surely want to live in. For criminal bullies there is no hiding place as forensic science enhances policing, ensuring convictions even decades later. Institutional bullying is a major embarrassment to the 21st century. But the signs are hopeful.

In schools there are anti bullying ambassadors, upstanders for marginalised children once left to fend for themselves. In the workplace, there are anti bullying helplines and free counselling. Judges are becoming streetwise as large numbers of litigants-in-person pass through Tribunals, defying toxic employers. Hopefully the days of the Dickensian bully-barrister are numbered. Community police and housing associations learned from the horrific murder of Bijan Ebrahimi. The time is ripe for the promotion of the moral upstander and the demise of the do-nothing bystander.

There are plenty of opportunities for bullies who wish to reform. Familial abuse happens less behind closed doors. Investigative Journalists in print, the radio and television work to expose injustices in a fair way, unlike infamous forbears at The News of the World. Change.org and 38 Degrees offer voiceless people an opportunity to speak out, for caring individuals to support them in droves and for well-supported petitions to reach Parliament, in a way previously not possible. Social media is imperfect, often working against itself to harm. Yet social media shines a light on social injustice in a way far more accessible than was possible in previous centuries.

So, what next? Deal with the basics first. Get support (vital). Get to know the major players and how they relate. Study human dynamics and how individuals and groups react, so that you know how to help turn a negative into a positive. Knowing why people act as they do is empowering; it gives an advantage. Next, understand yourself; the relationship between thinking, feeling and action. This was bread-and-butter for Roman Stoics and is brought up to date by psychologists as the 'triangle of insight.' You have a great deal of choice though you may not realize it. Study history and learn about moral panic, about how society changes and what causes those changes. Then study the snapshots and look at the role models (celebrities who overcame bullying at school is in Resources). Finally, take action.

Some strategies are common to all types of bullying, others for specific environments. Some will work for you and some may not but you will not know until you try. Make a personal commitment to change your behaviour and outfox the bully! Finally, look at books, film and websites in the resources section for ideas. Over to you!

* * *

SPACE FOR YOUR NOTES:

PERSPECTIVES

39: 'UNSURE WHAT BULLYING MEANS'

Nina

Nina was bullied at junior school. She remembers being excluded from team games which left her feeling sad and isolated. She was the butt of taunts about her lack of interest in sports and was dubbed, 'slow coach.' She had to wear glasses and for this crime was called, 'four eyes,' with pupils stealing her prescription glasses. Like many kids in the late 20th century she wore home-made clothing and was considered frumpy (by pupils whose parents could afford to buy them ready-made clothes) leading to taunts of, 'granny shoes.' She became classroom scapegoat, having pens flicked at her; the type of pen you dipped in a pot, resulting in her clothes being stained with ink.

Nina believes she was targeted because she 'showed weakness'. She compares herself with her husband who also wore glasses to school but was not bullied because he was, 'clever, sporty.' She told me girls were the worst bullies, trying at every opportunity to humiliate her. Although boys did bully her they would stop after a while whereas girls persisted. Like many pupils in the 1970's and 1980's she was targeted by teachers. For example, the PE (physical education) teacher would not allow her to be excused for games, including netball, though she knew Nina suffered with arthritis. This teacher also humiliated her, pointing out her glasses and causing other kids to laugh at Nina. Nina was last to be picked for games.

Nina was also bullied at work. In her first job, the boss made the girls clean a toilet wall with a toothbrush. He would fire staff for trivial offences, gaining a sense of power from this. She was part of a crowd bullied by another manager who would take money out of their wages if the float money was not right. At another job she was kept in the dark about house rules and no one would tell her when she could take breaks, she being too nervous to ask. She said this type of behaviour 'would repeat over the years.' But she didn't like to 'make a fuss.' When she found a job she liked, she was still experiencing bullying but as she was popular she decided to stick it out. Nina says she became more assertive over time and was heartened by one of the bullies apologising to her, though this was many years after the event.

I asked if there were upstanders and she told me some of the boys were supportive, giving her sound advice which lead to overt bullying stopping. However, gossiping from a distance continued. I asked Nina what she thought the bullies got out of their behaviour. She felt probably they did not understand the psychological impact on her and that it made them feel good. She believes bullying is a character trait. I asked if she was aware victims can become bullies and she said, yes, social awareness saved her from turning. She says the bullying had an impact on how she treats her children. She makes sure she listens and makes sure they can approach her any time with problems. She also looks out for signs of teasing and makes sure as far as possible that 'everyone is treated the same.' She says being bullied has not prevented her striving for and achieving her ambitions, however it is at the back of her mind and comes up when things happen to remind her.

* * *

SPACE FOR YOUR NOTES:

40: EXPERIENCES OF VICTIMS

Frank

Frank believes bullies target individuals who are 'different' to themselves. In his case he wore spectacles and outdated clothing. Around age seven he was beaten up by bullies and his possessions stolen or damaged. Retrieving his clothing made him late for classes then he received punishment from school, doubling his agony. He was often stressed in anticipation of being bullied. He says others appeared to enjoy his discomfort and this he vividly remembers years later. Of all the bullying he experienced he ranks it in order of the greatest fear:

1. psychological bullying
2. name calling
3. physical violence

He felt that in the 1970's bullying was expected to take place, though he knows it is less tolerated now. Even teachers would bully him, using ridicule, with pupils joining in by copying the teacher. He did not get much support from his family. His father worked in a nightclub so he got used to being told to 'get on with it'. He felt intimidated by his father and was brought up to believe the world a dangerous place and bullying was to be expected. However, when his parents confronted a teacher bully she was shocked when she realized what she had done. Once he bullied a fellow pupil who was quiet and disabled by a limp [*because of childhood arthritis*] but 40 years later Frank has not forgotten and is keen to apologise.

As a teenager he would intervene if he saw bullying going on so long as he did not fear reprisals, mainly psychological bullying which he could not easily deal with. He felt he became hard as a result of having little empathy when he was bullied and was resigned to it. Only later did he become angry about it. He says it gave him more empathy towards others and he always acts when his children report bullying. He has intervened on seeing parents verbally abusing their child. He feels the bullying shaped him, 'in a good way' but made him curious rather than 'better.' In his current post he has the power to deal with bullies and is keen to re-educate them.

Donald
Donald was bullied badly at school in the 1950's, physically and psychologically. His father did not understand, being a soldier who had a father who physically chastised him throughout childhood. The bullying affected his entire life leaving him wary and avoiding people. He lives alone, never married and has few friends, living an isolated existence in a social housing tower block where he rarely sees neighbours. Donald is bitter about the bullying and still angry at his treatment. Once he followed a youth who abused him, shouting insults from his motorbike before driving off. Incensed, Donald caught up with him at traffic lights, pulled him off his bike and hit him. Eventually Donald joined a Dojo where he learned Judo and Aikido. He was taught how to deal with situations without losing his temper and thus losing face. He became a brown belt in karate. He smiles when he says no one bullies him now. However, he remains isolated and believes this will never change.

Pamela
Pamela was ridiculed by teachers in 1960's, taunts about her size and 'foreign' accent. She was laughed at by the class and this still upsets her. She has forgiven these people because of her religious belief. She likes to encourage others who have been bullied not to give up but, like Pamela, develop skills and

talents. This gives her satisfaction. She remains over-sensitive to remarks about herself and others and wishes she could do something to prevent this. Pamela says she never learned to deal with bullies other than avoid them. This worked for her on a day-to-day basis but now she has kids of her own she is helping them find alternative strategies.

Fiona

'I remember a weak Manager who let a subordinate run rings around him. This Mental Nurse had been picking on me a long time and at that point in my career I did not have the nous to know what to do apart from telling her manager. Her behaviour included spreading malicious rumours, interrupting my present-ations with facetious comment, decrying my patient work and claiming I bullied her (classic bully ploy). The Psychiatrist said pointedly during a team meeting how she always left me out. In a group therapy session her Manager organised for the team, who were demoralised, she piped up in the long silence that I had, 'made a vicious and unprovoked attack' on her. I was speechless. No one said anything, not even the Psychologist who knew her from past experience. I wish I had had the guts to ask her to explain herself! Everyone sat heads down, leading the astonished Group Therapist to baldly ask who the Leader was – if we had one and perhaps we needed someone stronger. On one occasion the Nurse was talking about her sex life to a colleague whilst I was in the room. Glancing at me, she made a vulgar gesture, cupping one hand like a ring then pushing her finger through it whilst grinning at me. It seems she assumed I was naïve. This time I reported her to my Supervisor. At the next team meeting the Psychologist commented that the Nurse and I should talk about our relationship. Thinking it would do no good and feeling irked, I nevertheless agreed. But when *we were alone she spent the entire time criticising me, how I conducted myself and how qualified she was compared to me. As she left she smirked and said, 'I really enjoyed that. We must do it again.' I had had enough. I saw her in a corridor next morning and walked towards, shouldered her, pushing her hard against the wall. Her look of astonishment gave me a thrill. To this day I am glad what I did. When I saw her again I gave her eye contact, not aggressively but not leaving her gaze until she looked away. When she next interrupted me I screwed up my courage and said loudly that it was my turn. Again her Manager said nothing but the team looked on expectantly. This time she backed down. By this time I had seen signs of pain behind her eyes. I did not feel sorry for her because she never apologised. I believed then, and still do, receiving apology is a vital part of turnaround and must come before any forgiveness. This nurse left me pretty much alone after that, though occasionally I was informed of nasty things she'd said about me. I took no further action but pretty much ignored her. I stayed a year then left. Though I was to make the same mistake again, this time more drastically, I would advise anyone given similar circumstances to leave. There is little point staying where there are few signs of support in difficult times.'*

SPACE FOR YOUR NOTES:

41: HR MANAGER ON WORKPLACE BULLYING

James

James says he is glad there is zero tolerance for workplace bullying in most organisations. Bullying is sometimes known as victimisation, where the target becomes abused by a manager or colleagues, often for very little overt reason. The only staff protected by law are those who come under the Disability Discrimination Act, for example because of race, sexual orientation, disability or sexual preference. For victims to take a case to an Industrial Tribunal they have to have two years service, which leaves very new employees without protection. Bullying takes many forms. Many employees found themselves being pressed to do overtime which they do not want. Others were subjected to emotional blackmail, for example it is implied unless they do this or that they might lose their job, be demoted or refused promotion. He has deal with cases where managers shout at staff. He has dealt with confident subordinates bullying a less confident manager, refusing to do things especially if they are key to that area of work.

James says managers are often shocked when it is pointed out they have bullied an employee; 'it takes the wind out of their sails. They are shocked.' But rather than being sorry for their behaviour he says they feel challenged because of the potential punishment of job loss. He believes this behaviour often cannot be changed because the manager has some sort of personality disorder. James would like to see anti bullying training included in staff inductions. Larger firms often have Employee Assistance Programmes (EAP's) 'but smaller ones would find this expensive.'

* * *

SPACE FOR YOUR NOTES:

42: CHILDLINE OUTREACH WORKER

Jos

Jos was bullied at school. He was not only physically abused but subjected to name-calling and psychological abuse. He got very angry but this helped him recover over time. As he became more assertive the bullying stopped. When Childline began, he jumped at the chance of becoming a Childline volunteer. At Childline he was an outreach worker, interviewing parents and asking them to embrace the concept of Childline. Some parents were hostile, fearing what their children might say and not liking the idea of outsiders given information by their own kids. He found the work satisfying but said he was shocked how only half the calls got through because of a lack of volunteers, leaving call centre staff pressured.

(*There is now a national recruitment drive to employ more call handlers*).

* * *

SPACE FOR YOUR NOTES:

43: CELEBRITIES WHO WERE BULLIED AT SCHOOL

And now more encouragement! Many successful people were once bullied at school but went on to have good careers, developing talents and skills they never knew they had during their awful school years. Not every victim becomes a celebrity but their stories are empowering. It proves bullying can happen to anyone, not because (as is falsely believed) the victim is weak or inadequate. Search online for these names and read their stories:

Recovered Victims of Childhood Bullying.
Jessica Alba
Victoria Beckham
Pierce Brosnan
Sandra Bullock
Catherine, Duchess of Cambridge
Bill Clinton
Tom Cruise
Eminem
Lady Gaga
Madonna
Barack Obama
Michael Phelps
Daniel Radcliffe
Rihanna
Winona Ryder
Stephen Spielberg
Howard Stern
George Takei
Justin Timberlake
Emma Watson
Kate Winslet
Tiger Woods

RESOURCES

44: BOOKS / FILM

The following material contains themes of bullying and empowerment. When people decry fiction for insight into everyday life issues, remember films and novels are written after extensive research and frequently based on fact. Human experience at base is very similar. How often have you recognised real life situations from films, books or documentaries?

Books – Classic Fiction
1984 – George Orwell (dystopia)
Dr Jekyll and Mr Hyde – Robert Louis Stevenson
King Richard III – William Shakespeare play
Lolita – Vladimir Nabokov
Lord of the Flies – William Golding
Nicholas Nickleby – Charles Dickens
Sherlock Holmes (various) – Sir Arthur Conan Doyle:
   Moriarty [character], 'the Napoleon of crime' (sociopath):
   The Valley of Fear
   The Final Problem
The Martian Chronicles – Ray Bradbury
The Mayor of Casterbridge – Thomas Hardy
This Be the Verse – poem by Philip Larkin
Tom Brown's Schooldays – (child abuse at public school)

Books – Fiction
44 Scotland Street – Alexander McCall Smith [Bruce, narcissist]
Bad Girls – Jacqueline Wilson

Carrie – Stephen King
Silence of the Lambs – Thomas Harris

Books – Non Fiction
Blaming the Victim – William Ryan
Bully Insight – Tim Field
Bully Proof Kids – Stella O'Malley, ISBN 978-0-7171-7542-0
Kilvert's Diary – Robert Francis Kilvert
Cynthia Payne, The Life & Work of an English Madam – Cynthia
   Payne
Man's Search for Meaning – Carl Jung
Psychological Social Stages of Human Development- Erik
   Erickson
Queen Bees & Wannabees – Rosalind Wiseman
Snakes in Suits: When Psychopaths Go to Work – Robert Hare
The Daily Stoic – Ryan Holliday
The Daily Stoic Journal – Ryan Holliday
The Bird Man of Alcatraz – Thomas E Gaddis
The Fatal Shore – Robert Hughes [Australian penal colonies]
The Lost Child of Philomena Lee – Martin Sixsmith
The Miracle of Mindfulness – Thitch Nat Hanh
The Psychopath Inside – James Fallon

Classic Film
All About Eve
Boys Town – will a bully reform to save other boys from a life
   in prison?
Dr Jekyll and Mr Hyde (evil/good in one person)
Frankenstein – Doctor Frankenstein creates a monster he cannot
   control
Goodnight Mr Tom (child abuse and redemption)
Hush, Hush Sweet Charlotte (child abuse)

Jane Eyre (child abuse and redemption)
The History of Mr Polly (wife abuse)
The Illusionist (sexually abusive relationship & redemption)
The Secret Garden (isolated family find redemption)
The Suspicions of Mr Whicher (sibling child murder)
To Kill a Mockingbird (racial abuse)
Whatever Happened to Baby Jane (child abuse)

Film
About a Boy
Billy Elliot (empowerment)
Bully (bullycide)
Carrie (revenge on bullies)
Cyberbully
Fistful of Dollars (family warfare)
La Vie En Rose (abused child finds redemption – story of Edith
   Piaf)
Lord of the Flies (breakdown of social ties under duress)
Matilda (moral drama; result of childhood lies)
Mean Girls (bullying)
Mildred Pierce (family abuse)
Mommy Dead and Dearest (Munchausen by Proxy)
Philomena (search for her long-lost child by an Irish teenage
   mother)
Shawshank Redemption (wife murder and redemption)
Shine (child abuse & redemption – story of David Helfgott)
The Bird Man of Alcatraz (sociopath redeemed through
   ornithology)
The Colour Purple (child sexual abuse)
The Dead Poet's Society (empowerment)
The Private Life of Bees (child sexual abuse)

* * *

45: ENQUIRIES, ORGANISATIONS, WEBSITES

- HELP AGENCIES (alphabetical)
- Miscellaneous information

HELP AGENCIES (alphabetical)
anti bullying websites & campaign organisations
http://www.bullybusters.org.uk
http://www.bullying.co.uk
http://bullyonline.org/index.php tim field's charity
http://www.change.org
ditch the label
http://www.familylives.org.uk
internet matters
http://www.38degrees.org

....

AVoice (Advocacy for victims of crime who need support)
Freephone 0800 254 0777
Internet@ www.thecareforum.org
Email@ Avoice@thecareforum.org,uk

Role:
- those with learning disability, mental health problems, need support due to age, ethnicity, gender, religious belief.
- help understand legal process
- look at options
- help with support from other agencies
- offer information and guidance
Tel: 0800 1111

Available for help on family & sexual violence, incest, sexting.

....

Childline
24 telephone support & Advice for children/teenagers
Tel: 0800 1111

- nb calls to advice line DO NOT show on phone or bills for landlines
- Ditto for certain mobiles (check with call handler)

Offer:
- telephone call, email, 1-2-1 chat with advisor
- message boards to share fears & information
- reassurance and support
- advice about dealing with abuse

....

Community Police – anti-social behaviours (ASB)
Report hate crime/anti-social behaviour: 101
report hate crime online: www.report-it.org.uk

Role:
- keeping peace in the community
- Investigate Criminal anti-social behaviours
- Investigate domestic /sexual violence
- Investigate trafficking/ modern slavery

....

Refuge See also Women's aid.

Women's helpline : 0808 2000 247
Email: helpline@womensaid.org.uk

Men's helpline: 0808 801 0327
Men's web chat: Thursdays 10 – 4pm

Deal with:
- domestic/sexual violence
- honour violence
- trafficking / modern slavery
- female genital mutilation

Services:
- 24 hour helplines
- women's helpline operated by women
- refer callers to local safe accommodation (refuges)

- refer callers to local professionals via drop-in services
- refuges take women alone or with their children
- help with safety & crisis planning
- offer emotional support

....

SARI – 'Stand Against Racism & Inequality'
Web: www.sariweb.org.uk
email sari@sariweb.org.uk

Deal with:
- hate crime
- support over feelings and mental state
- look at options for taking action
- coordinate with other agencies and check on their progress
- offer support through legal proceedings
- help with making complaints
- educational service to schools, youth agencies, businesses etc
- educate on diversity, conflict resolution

The Red Balloon Centre Cambridge.
School for bullied & traumatised children

http://www.bbc.co.uk/news/av/stories-42254524/the-school-for-bullied-and-traumatised-children

....

Victim Support (referral via Community Police)
Support line: 08 08 16 89 111
Next Generation Text line: 18001 08081689111
online – http://www.victimsupport.org.uk
Twitter – @VictimSupport
Facebook – VictimSupport

Offer:
- access direct or via police
- provide advice and emotional support by trained counsellor
- provide access to other help organisations

- access to potential compensation / financial help
- provide access to means to secure your home
- accompany and support through any court procedures
- provide interpreters
- available ANY TIME (during or after crime)

Women's Aid (see also Refuge helpline)
Provide local Refuge shelters & support for women & children

Offer:
- 180 local refuges for women & their children
- train professionals & help agencies
- raise public awareness of domestic violence
- conduct research
- campaign

MISCELLANEOUS INFORMATION

Leaflets on: The Anti-Social Behaviour, Crime & Policing Act 2014:

www.gov.uk/.../anti-social-behaviour-crime-and-police-bill

Hate crime: https://www.cps.gov.uk/hate-crime

Podcast on toxic workplaces: http://rootsofempathy.org/ and
https://bibr.org/podcast/2018/-05/toxic_workplaces

useful dictionary of modern, urban terminology:
http://www.urbandictionary.com

dealing with anxiety & panic attack [free online course]:
http://www.panic-attacks.co.uk/course

Professor Nathan Lento: future development of mankind:
thehumanevolutionblog.com

about adrenaline, testosterone and other hormones: http://www.
yourhormonesinfo/hormones

GLOSSARY

anti-social behaviour (ASB)	behaviour which upsets others in the community – much of which now constitutes a criminal offence
bait out [cyber bullying]	websites whiich encourage illegal posting of sexual images or gossip, where the victim is unaware this is happening
blacklisting	method used to covertly exclude professionals from their work
bullycide	suicide attributed to a causal factor of bullying
cat fishing [cyber bullying]	using false identity to lure someone into a long relationship
causal factor	one of several factors contributing to any particular event
Chinese Whispers	malicious gossip which changes as it spreads
cry bully	a bully who masquerades as a victim, to humiliate the target
cyber bullying	bullying conducted via the internet using any electronic device
cyber stalking	following someone around the internet [cf stalking]
deflected action	damaging property of a victim – symbolic of hurting them
Degeneracy (now discredited)	theory of Benedict Morel (1809 – 1873): families show stages of a downward spiral which he outlined as: alcohol and opiate addiction; prostitution & sexual degeneracy; criminality; insanity; imbecility; sterility.
depression	type of mental illness marked by pervasive low mood.

dissing [cyber bullying]	posting cruel or humiliating images of a victim online
duvet day	faking illness to get a day off. duvet days are recognised in the US as a form of stress relief and is accepted by firms
dynamic	a process that is constantly changing [in flux]
EAP	Employee Assistance Programme – workplace counselling
entropy	gradual degeneration, over time, of organics & non organics
Eugenics (now discredited)	false science which sought to prove certain races superior
fake profile	someone who masquerades online, to falsely obtain a gain
familial abuse	sexual abuse in a family; also incest or forced incest
filibustering	[parliament] mp speaking non stop, to prevent another mp speaking [one mp cannot interrupt another who is standing]
flaming	deliberately provoking an argument online
Flashman	Bully in 'Tom Brown's Schooldays'
forced incest	siblings forced to have sexual relations by an abuser
fraping [cyber bullying]	illegally changing details on someone's social media account
'good boy [girl]'	someone who does something only for personal gain
grooming [cyber bullying]	paedophiles luring under age kids for sex through falsehoods
halo effect (the)	first impressions stick, even in the face of counter evidence i.e. perceived 'goddess' or 'devil' despite evidence of contrary
hate crime	disability discrimination in law for certain protected classes
intranet	an internal internet used by modern large firms
ISP	Internet Service Provider

Lightbox	Device for viewing slides when the larger
macrocosm/microcosm	picture reflects the small scale equivalent
mindfulness	type of meditation, staying 'in the moment' [present]
moral panic	group of individuals taking against a particular social cause
Peephole viewer	Spy hole in door of Victorian brothel
personality disorder	characteristics (in psychiatry) depicting character problems
phrenology [discredited]	claim of detecting character through bumps in skull
power games	psychological abuse against someone more vulnerable
projection & splitting	attributing bad traits of one person onto a victim, whilst the perpetrator is seen as perfect, see also halo effect
protagonist	the person who begins a particular chain of action
protected characteristics	about hate crime – categories which are protected by law
sexting [cyber bullying]	[sexual shaming]: posting sexual images of someone else without permission, in order to humiliate
stroking [TA}	rewarding for 'good' behaviour [Berne, transactional analysis]
talking cure	counselling etc. term coined by Freud's patient, Anna O
toxic environment	firm or organisation marked by fear, gossip & bullying
trickery [cyber bullying]	assuming a false online identity (impersonation) for gain
trolls [cyber bullying]	following someone covertly using the internet cf stalking
zero hours contract	a worker is not paid when not called in for work but expected to be available at all times in case called in

INDEX